THE PAPER DOLL PRINCESS

Walking As a New Creation

BONNY ALLEN IBARRA

"Therefore, if anyone is in Christ, he is a new creation;
the old has gone, the new has come!"
2 Corinthians 5:17

INTRODUCTION

We sometimes tend to read over verses like this, not really stopping to take hold of all of the amazing truths expressed by them. For example, this remarkable verse found in 2 Corinthians 5:17 tells us that something inside of you and I was eternally transformed when we were saved. I have read this verse many times, as well as others that talk about the spiritual transformation that occurs in a new believer at salvation. I have to admit, however, that after a lifetime of Sunday sermons, I realized one day that I really had not heard much teaching on the subject; and, as a seasoned believer, I found myself at a loss to explain some of the most basic and profound truths associated with the gospel of Jesus Christ.

In other words, if someone stopped to ask me if I was a new creation in Christ, I would boldly announce with certainty, "Yes!" If someone asked if I was reborn, with great confidence I would acknowledge that I am in fact a reborn child of God; however, if pressed with the questions, "How were you made new?", "What was made new?", or "What does it mean to be reborn or born again?", I would likely have muttered through some sort of garbled answer, trying to sound more intelligent on the subject than I really was.

A few years back, I felt drawn by the Holy Spirit to study the answers to these important questions simply using the Bible as my resource. The journey has been truly amazing, and the answers I found have completely transformed the way I live out my own Christian life on this earth. I began to realize that though I had found the gospel for salvation early in my childhood, I had missed much of the power of the gospel as it pertains to my daily life. Though I knew with certainty that I was a reborn, new creation of the Most High God, my lack of understanding of the full impact of these gospel terms kept me spiritually handicapped for how to truly walk as such.

I have written this book because I believe that, like me, many in the church have become spiritually crippled in how to deal with fleshly issues because we have not understood that the gospel, or "good news" of Jesus Christ, was not intended to end at salvation, but rather to begin. The gospel is meant to be applied to every minute of every day, in every situation of our lives. It is meant to impact us in a supernatural way in every thought, word, and deed. It is meant to change us from the inside out. The gospel empowers us for genuine righteousness and holiness, and it enables us to live a truly rich and abundant life.

In this book, we will explore God's original design for us, the consequences to both our body and our spirit after the fall, the transformation that occurs in each of us when we put our full confidence and trust in the blood of Christ for salvation, and finally, the completed work we will experience in eternity. Practically, we will examine the implications of those changes and how they impact our continued walk with God while in this body.

It is my prayer, and the goal of this book, that the reader will walk away with a mind renewed in the truth of his or her personal spiritual transformation and true spiritual identity; and then with that understanding, the believer will find a whole new arsenal of weapons with which to fight the good fight of faith.

DEDICATION

To my loving spouse and ideal partner for life, Richard Ibarra.
You bless me every day with your overwhelming
support and encouragement.

ACKNOWLEDGMENTS

———— ❧ ————

I have a child who gained 41 lbs, grew 10 inches taller, and aged more than 3 years from the time I started writing this book. Calvin, you are the most amazing and patient kid I have ever known. I am so thankful for the opportunity to be your mom and for your love and sweet spirit. I can hardly wait to see God's plans unfold for your life.

Thank you to my Dad, Calvin Allen, and Mom, Carmen Allen, for introducing me to the love of Christ at an early age and for teaching me that it's ok to color outside the lines at times.

Thank you to the beautiful and talented Tamara Allen for your labor in editing and proof-reading my manuscript. Your support and love mean so much to me.

I would like to give a very special thanks to my amazing illustrator, Ashley Marie Drennan. Your time and talents are so appreciated. You brought this vision to life.

In addition, I would like to thank the many other dear friends and loved ones who have allowed me to ramble incessantly about my book, those who offered support, comments, and feedback, and those who assisted in the processes of editing, proofreading, and design. Your encouragement and support to go the distance has meant the world to me. There are too many of you to name, but know that I love and appreciate every one of you.

CONTENTS

CONTENTS

FOREWORD

One day, I was sitting in a weekend gathering of believers in a foreign country watching a friend be ordained into a new pastoral position. Suddenly, my thoughts were flooded with what I would best describe as a type of "download" related to a new ministry direction called The Paper Doll Princess. In a nutshell, the idea was to use life-size paper dolls to illustrate foundational Biblical truths that occur in a person before, during, and after salvation. Immediately, countless scriptures began pouring into my mind about the various articles of spiritual clothing represented in the Word of God and the incredible amount of instruction by God to His people to "Put them on."

As we arrived home that day, I could hardly wait to share this remarkable experience with my sweet husband, fully anticipating that he would get equally as excited about it as I was. His initial response deflated me, "What in the world do paper dolls and princesses have in common with a woman of God?"

A paper doll is fragile and typically carries very little value. It might look nice for a little while, but if you play with it for any length of time, it simply will wear out and disintegrate into a crumpled up mess. A princess, on the other hand, is priceless.

The paper doll represents our fallen flesh, or physical body. Like a paper doll, it is simply a vessel made of dust that is to be used up, worn out, and discarded in due time (Gen. 3:19; Ps. 104:29). Frequently, though, we place our identity in it. We sense that it is fallen and corrupt, so we attempt to cover up its flaws by accessorizing it with make-up, pretty shoes, and sparkly jewels. Then, we present it to God as if He might take some pride or pleasure in it. However, even after giving it all the attention we can afford, its basic properties remain the same. It is still ... dust.

Our spiritual identity, however, is not in the paper. This piece of paper is not who we are in the Lord. Our broken flesh has never had the power or ability to please God, and it never will. For now, it is simply an instrument that we can choose to use for God's righteous purposes while we live on this Earth (Romans 6:13; Eph. 2:10).

Eventually, this body will go to the grave and return to dust. We do not need to be discouraged by this fact because the Word of God says that God is preparing for each of us a perfect new body as part of our future inheritance (2 Cor. 5:1-5).

So, while we live on the earth in this fallen body, we must be reminded that our true spiritual identity lies not in the paper, but in the reality of who we are as spirit – that new creation that we became when we were born-again as righteous daughters of the living God. We are royal Princesses in His Kingdom, unique children born of the King of Kings, and Lord of Lords. As such, we hold the most intrinsic value to our heavenly Father.

Our Father loves to dress us up, and He has provided us with a brand new designer wardrobe. We desperately needed this new wardrobe because our old worn out clothes were seen by our Father as "filthy rags" (Isaiah 64:6). Our Father's word tells us that He has clothed us with garments of salvation, and that He has given us His very own robe of righteousness (Isaiah 61:10). He tells us to put on the armor of light and to clothe ourselves with the Lord Jesus (Romans 13:12-14). He tells us that we are to renew our minds daily by taking off our old self and by putting on the new self (Eph. 4:22-23). This new wardrobe is His free gift to us, not because we pleased Him, but because of His amazing grace and His sincere love for us. Our Father delights in seeing us wear our new clothes.

Did you know, however, that there are days that for some reason, we still seek comfort in our old familiar filthy rags? Though we have the most beautiful wardrobe given to us by the

King Himself, we choose to go back and put on our own way of righteousness. Blinded to the reality of our appalling exterior, we come and parade ourselves in front of Him as if saying, "Father, do you like it? Am I pretty?" Can you imagine His regret at our choice of garments?

Yes, we are still paper dolls for now. A day is soon coming, however, when our paper features will all disappear. What will remain is lasting and eternal. In hope, we can look forward to that day when we will share a blessed eternity with our heavenly Father in His glorious Kingdom. This is our reality. The rest is simply an illusion.

"...for when you eat of it, you will surely die."
Genesis 2:17(b)

CHAPTER 1

ONCE UPON A TIME, IN A LAND FAR, FAR AWAY ...

*I*n fiction-based literature, many of the greatest chronicles ever written grandly articulate the story of a beautiful princess who has somehow, through extraordinary circumstances, lost her royal position. Her epic saga classically begins with "Once upon a time," and most frequently ends with the famous "happily ever after." Her interim struggle includes a villain who serves to facilitate the detrimental loss of her noble identity. It includes a time of introspective discovery and recognition of her loss, aided by the timely arrival of a helper. Her story climaxes with the selfless sacrifice of a loving rescuer, resulting in an intensely powerful, personal metamorphosis that ultimately enables her to once again repossess her true identity and royal position. The villain is defeated, and his power over her is lost. That which he craftily intended to destroy her, in the end, is that which ultimately enables her to receive the truest riches of abundant life: the greatest treasure found in genuine character, humility, gratitude, selflessness, faithfulness, relational love, and authentic fellowship.

The stories of these renowned characters of old are not unlike our own spiritual journey. As a matter of fact, I believe many of these famous fairy tales were written to illustrate the most profound spiritual truths related to our own transformation in Christ. Like their stories, our own chronicle can only be fully understood as we look deeply into the truth of our own origins, the depths of our great loss, the selfless sacrificial love of our rescuing redeemer, and the extraordinary circumstances that enable our transformations along the way.

The Setting: Life Before the Fall

Our narrative begins in the most beautiful and perfect of settings called the Garden of Eden. By the breath of His mouth, the Almighty God brought forth the sun, moon, stars, planets, and galaxies. By His own word, He established the earth and everything in it. At the end of each day, He looked at His new kingdom and in a word summed up His creation as "Good." Have you ever thought about how amazing that fresh new world must have been? It was untainted by sin and wholly free from sorrow, pain, suffering, grief, and death. Everything existed in perfect harmony, bringing the most wonderful glory to its Creator. The Bible says that on the sixth day, God created man. Once more, God looked upon the entirety of His creation and made the bold proclamation that it is not just "Good," but "Very good!"

Genesis 2:7 tells us that Adam's body was *formed* out of the dust of the ground. Take a moment here to imagine the tenderness of God's hand upon this very special part of His creation. The original Hebrew word for *formed* carries with it the idea of the work of a skillful potter or artisan.[a] After God formed Adam's body, He breathed into Adam's nostrils the breath of life, and Adam became a living being. I've often wondered if perhaps Adam, when he first opened His eyes, found himself sitting in the powerful hand of the Almighty, and staring into the tender, loving eyes of his Creator.

The "breath of life" that God breathed into Adam is the Hebrew word *"ruach,"* which is translated as *spirit* in other contexts. The Hebrew word for "living being" is *nephesh,* which is also translated as the word "soul." Notice, it is the addition of the breath of God, or the spirit, that made man a living being or soul. James

2:26 tells us that the body without the spirit is dead. Therefore, for the body to be a living being, the spirit must be present.

There was something especially unique about the creation of man that separated him from the rest of God's creation. No other creature is said to have become a living being by the breath of God. In this way, man is uniquely different from the rest of the animal world. Furthermore, in the opening pages of scripture, we learn that we were purposefully created to be image bearers of the eternal God on this earth. The fact that our original design by God was to bear His image is an important point to note because we will continue to encounter this phrase "in the image of," or "in the likeness of," as we further delve into understanding the process of our own spiritual transformation.

Other passages in scripture also equate the spirit of a man with the life-giving breath of God:

Job 32:8 - But it is the spirit in a man, the breath of the Almighty, that gives him understanding.

Job 33:4 - The Spirit of God has made me; the breath of the Almighty gives me life.

Job 34:13-15 - [13] Who appointed Him over the earth? Who put him in charge of the whole world? [14] If it were his intention and he withdrew his spirit and breath, [15] all mankind would perish together and man would return to the dust.

Isaiah 57:16 - I will not accuse forever, nor will I always be angry, for then the spirit of man would grow faint before me— the breath of man that I have created.

What else do we know about Adam and Eve's life before the fall? Genesis 2:25 tells us that "they were naked, and they felt no shame." Then Genesis 3:8 articulates that they "heard the sound of the Lord God as He was walking in the garden in the cool of the day." In the garden, one can easily presume that Adam and Eve enjoyed an intensely personal and intimate fellowship with their Creator. Their complete freedom from guilt and shame enabled them to walk and talk openly with God. During this time of deep intense fellowship with God, they experienced the truly rich and abundant life God had designed for them to enjoy. They were free, alive, and vibrant in ways we cannot likely imagine.

Before sin entered the world, there was no reason for Adam and Eve to be separated from God. Their body and their spirit had been born, or created, directly from God and were both created in His astounding image. Because of this, their body and spirit existed in perfect agreement with each other, and in agreement with God.

The illustration shown on the following page shows the purity of both their body and spirit at the time of their creation.

CREATED SOUL
Body & Spirit Perfectly Created in God's Image

The Conflict: Death After the Fall

God gave Adam and Eve one limitation or command. They could eat from the Tree of Life and all the beautiful trees in the garden, except one: the Tree of the Knowledge of Good and Evil. God instructed them not to eat of this tree, saying "for *when* you eat of it, *you will surely die*" (Gen. 2:17). We know that at some point after that, Adam and Eve disobeyed God and ate from this tree. Obviously, when they ate of it, they did not die in the direct sense of ceasing to exist because we know Adam went on to produce children and lived to the ripe old age of 930 years. Therefore,

God's definition of *death* in Genesis 2:17 must be broader. So, the question that we first must consider is this: "What died, or in what way did they die?"

What we know, from scripture, is that in the moment Adam and Eve disobeyed God by eating from the Tree of the Knowledge of Good and Evil, sin and death began to reign. Sin, now taking up legal residence within them both physically and spiritually, became the primary dominating force of power and control. The rich, vibrant, and abundant life they had formerly enjoyed, both in body and spirit, ceased to exist as they had known it.

In regard to the body, we know they began to age. Their bodies became susceptible to sickness, disease, pain, suffering, and eventually physical death. Furthermore, their bodies began to experience unnatural cravings, lust, and passions that were contrary to the righteous nature in which God had originally created them.

The death of their spirit was the same. Like the body, their spirit was given over to rebellion and depravity. Their spiritual minds became dark and twisted and grew increasingly hostile toward God (Romans 1:18-32).

Scripture tells us that all of humanity that followed inherited Adam's brokenness, his relationship as a slave to sin, and the impending physical and spiritual death that comes as a result of that enslavement.

Romans 5:12 - Therefore, just as sin entered the world through one man, and death through sin, and in this way death came to all men, because all sinned ...

The result of sin was that the pure relationship between God and His creation was broken; and therefore, God's intense, holy presence could only be experienced in part from a great distance under just the right circumstances. Though man once had walked in continuous fellowship and communion with his Creator, he was now separated from God and without hope. As a result, Adam, and those born after him, became the object of God's wrath and His righteous judgment.

BROKEN SOUL IN ADAM
Body & Spirit Broken and Enslaved to Sin

The illustration on the preceding page reveals the transformation to our body and spirit after the fall, and the reality that both are born broken, enslaved to sin, and separated from God.

The Bible records that when they sinned, the *eyes of both of them were opened.* They realized they were naked, so they sewed fig leaves together and made coverings for themselves; and then they hid from God (Gen. 3:7-8).

When their *eyes were opened,* what did they see? The name of the tree from which they ate indicates that they were exposed to the realities of darkness and evil, to morality and immorality, to moral law and ensuing justice. As a result, for the first time since the creation, they felt fear, guilt, and shame before their Maker.

Notice the aspect of clothing represented here in the garden. Because of the experience of guilt and shame, Adam and Eve tried to cover themselves by fashioning their own clothing to satisfy their guilt before God. It is significant to note that the habitual pattern of fallen flesh is to try to make its own garment to cover guilt and shame before God. Both believers and non-believers today still experience this same pattern of the flesh. Perhaps, we hide ourselves under the cloak of religious activity, or we put on the filthy rags of our own righteousness, wearing our own good deeds generated through self-effort to cover our guilt. Perhaps, we put on the hat of moral comparison, relatively measuring the perceived weight of our own sin against the sins of another. God demonstrated in the garden that our own provision of clothing was insufficient in His eyes. Nevertheless, we learn in Genesis 3:21, God had His own plan for covering Adam and Eve, just as He has for covering us today.

Genesis 3:21 - The Lord God made garments of skin for Adam and his wife and clothed them.

This is the first of many references in Scripture of the spiritual clothing that God provides for His children. This clothing, however, was very significant because it demonstrated that God Almighty already had a plan for how He would cover their sin and the sin of all broken humanity that followed. God's plan for covering sin would involve an amazing sacrifice by a willing party: the sacrifice of an innocent body and the shedding of innocent blood.

*"'The Redeemer will come to Zion, to those in Jacob
who repent of their sins,' declares the* Lord.*"*
Isaiah 59:20

CHAPTER 2

THE KINSMAN-REDEEMER

⸻⸻❧⸻⸻

*T*he Bible tells us that before we knew Christ, we walked
without hope and without God (Eph. 2:12). God loved
us, however, and wanted to provide a way for us to be reunited with
Him in a living, thriving relationship. Jesus declares in John 10:10,
"The thief comes only to steal and kill and destroy; I have come that
they may have *life*, and have it to the full (or abundantly)."

Throughout the next few chapters of this book, we will explore
the plan of God to return the abundant life to us that was once
experienced in the garden before the fall. The end of our separation from God begins with a legal process called Redemption.

Old Testament scripture spoke over and over about a future

Messiah that would come to redeem God's people. The Israelites

had been promised a redeemer; one whom they expected would

come and rescue them from earthly bondage and oppression.

> **Isaiah 62:11-12 -** [11] The Lord has made a proclamation to
> the ends of the earth; "Say to the Daughter of Zion, See
> your Savior comes! See, his reward is with him, and his
> recompense accompanies him. [12] They will be called the
> Holy People, *the Redeemed of the Lord.* And you will be
> called "sought after," the City no longer Deserted.

The people of God, the Jewish people known as "Israel," were

eagerly awaiting the coming of this Redeeming Messiah. In the

opening pages of New Testament scripture, Luke writes of the

prophetic song that Zachariah sang when his son, John the Baptist,

was born.

> **Luke 1:68-70 -** [68] Praise be to the Lord, the God of Israel,
> because he has come and *has redeemed his people.* [69] He
> has raised up a horn of salvation for us in the house of his
> servant David [70] (as he said through his holy prophets of
> long ago)

Luke also writes of the day that Joseph and Mary took Jesus to

be circumcised. While they were in the temple, Joseph and Mary

encountered a prophetess named Anna. Anna was eighty-four

years old and had been a widow for most of her life, dedicating herself to service in the temple. Luke 2:38 says that when she saw the baby, she gave thanks to God and spoke about the child to all who were looking forward to the *redemption* of Jerusalem.

Redemption was a familiar topic of discussion to the Jewish people. It was something for which they sought with great anticipation and eagerness. In their minds, the idea of redemption meant being freed from long-term enslavement and tyranny by their oppressors; yet, they also understood redemption as a legal term. Old Testament writings used this term in the context of legally freeing someone from slavery by payment of a ransom, or legally redeeming the land of inheritance back to its original owner (Leviticus 25:25-34; 27:14-33; Ruth 4:3-10).

What does REDEMPTION actually mean?

The word "REDEMPTION" is more than just the forgiveness or clearing of a debt. Redemption involves a legal transaction, and it literally means "to purchase back something that has been lost by the payment of a ransom."[a] For redemption to occur, several steps must take place.

Step 1 - Something must be lost.

Before redemption becomes a necessity, something first must be lost. This loss happens through death, enslavement, selling it, or giving it away through a legal transaction.

As we have already learned in Chapter 1, this is exactly what happened to us when the intimate fellowship with our Creator was broken, and the abundant life, which we once had enjoyed in the garden, was lost the moment that Adam and Eve disobeyed God. Romans 5:12-21 teaches us that because of Adam's disobedience, sin entered the world, and that sin brought condemnation, judgment, and death to all men. By Adam's sin, we all were made sinners.

Step 2 - Someone must be willing to pay a legal ransom price to redeem it.

In order for redemption to legally occur, a willing party with a legal right must come forward to pay the established price to redeem what is lost. We see this exemplified in the Old Testament story of Ruth and Boaz. Boaz was her kinsmen-redeemer. He not only had a legal right to redeem her and her property, but he was also willing to do it. There are many examples and laws governing the legal rights of redemption found in scripture.

Though the Israelites understood the legal process of redemption, they were looking for an earthly deliverer. As a result, many Jews misunderstood the Messiah's true purpose. The redemption which the prophets had foretold for them was much bigger than they ever anticipated, and it extended far beyond their own culture and experience. This Redeemer was good news of great joy "for all the people" (Luke 2:10). His redemption plan would be applied to the entire world.

To this day, many Jewish people are still waiting on an earthly Messiah to deliver them. They have missed the truth that Jesus was their redeeming Messiah, not understanding that His work of redemption was much broader than their own earthly expectations.

In speaking of the birth of Jesus, John testifies that the true light that gives light to every man was coming into the world, yet the world did not recognize Him. His own people did not receive Him (John 1:9-14). When He died on the cross, those who had put their hope in Him as their redeeming Messiah were both confounded and disappointed at His death because He did not fulfill their earthly expectations of the Messiah (Luke 24:15-27). There is no question that the Jewish people of that day understood the Messiah was to be a redeemer; however, what they did not understand was the true extent of what He came to redeem, nor the price that would be required of Him to redeem it.

Isaiah 53 is one of many Old Testament prophesies describing the life, death, and purpose of the Messiah that was to come. It was written over 700 years before Jesus' birth. After predicting astonishingly accurate details about the sufferings and crucifixion of Christ, verse 10 says:

Isaiah 53:10 - Yet it was the Lord's will to crush him and cause him to suffer, and though the Lord makes his life a guilt offering, he will see his offspring and prolong his days, and the will of the Lord will prosper in his hand.

Before Christ's death, the law required a guilt offering to be presented to God to atone for, or cover, the sins of the people. This offering could only temporarily appease God's wrath against their sin, yet it had no power to change their broken condition. Hebrews 10:1-10 confirms this:

Hebrews 10:1-10 - [1] The law is only a shadow of the good things that are coming—not the realities themselves. For this reason it can never, by the same sacrifices repeated endlessly year after year, make perfect those who draw near to worship. [2] If it could, would they not have stopped being offered? For the worshipers would have been cleansed once for all, and would no longer have felt guilty for their sins. [3] But those sacrifices are an annual reminder of sins, [4] because *it is impossible for the blood of bulls and goats to take away sins.* [5] Therefore, **when Christ came into the world**, he said:

"Sacrifice and offering you did not desire, but a body you prepared for me; [6] with burnt offerings and sin offerings you were not pleased. [7] Then I said, 'Here I am—it is written about me in the scroll— I have come to do your will, O God.' "

[8] First he said, "Sacrifices and offerings, burnt offerings and sin offerings you did not desire, nor were you pleased with them" (although the law required them to be made).

⁹ Then he said, "Here I **am**, I have come to do your will." He sets aside the first to establish the second. ¹⁰ And by *that will*, we have been made holy through the sacrifice of the body of Jesus Christ once for all.

Notice that this conversation between God the Father and His son, Jesus, or *Yahweh*, occurred *"when Christ came into the world."* In this conversation, Jesus affirms that God's wrath and righteous justice were not satisfied by the routine sacrifices required under the Mosaic Law. Then Jesus says something very interesting, *"...but, a body you prepared for me."* This short phrase tells us that it was God the Father's plan to send His son. Lest we ever question our Father's heartfelt, uncontaminated love for us, we must realize that it is He who prepared Christ's body, which was destined to become the final sacrifice and guilt offering for our sin. Jesus agreed to the Father's will, and it is through the Father's will that we have been made holy.

Step 3 - The ransom price must be paid.

This may seem obvious, but the process of redemption is not complete unless the willing party actually pays the *full price* the ransom demands. Otherwise, the process of redemption is legally rendered null and void.

In Paul's letter to the Romans, he tells us that we all have sinned and fallen short of the glory of God, but we are all also justified freely by His grace through the "REDEMPTION" that came by Jesus Christ.

> **Romans 3:21-24** - [21] But now a righteousness from God, apart from law, has been made known, to which the Law and the Prophets testify. [22] This righteousness from God comes through faith in Jesus Christ to all who believe. There is no difference, [23] for all have sinned and fall short of the glory of God, [24] and are justified freely by his grace *through the redemption that came by Christ Jesus.*

The word "justify" is also a legal term. It means to be legally judged as one who is righteous and worthy of salvation.[a] Paul continues this passage in Romans by explaining the reason God chose to redeem us in this manner.

> **Romans 3:25-26** - [25] God (*the Father*) presented him (*Jesus*) as a sacrifice of atonement, through faith in his blood. He *(the Father)* did this to demonstrate his *(the Father's)* justice, because in his forbearance he had left the sins committed beforehand unpunished— [26] he did it to demonstrate his justice at the present time, so as to be just and the one who justifies those who have faith in Jesus.

Here we read again that it was God the Father who presented Jesus as a sacrifice of atonement. The word atonement means "to appease."[a] This means that it was the Father's idea to send Jesus as a sacrifice to take away sin so that His own wrath against sin would be appeased. This "atonement" was done through the shedding

of the innocent blood of Jesus Christ, the perfect Lamb o
who takes away the sins of the world. At the cross, part three of
the redemption process was finished. The price to purchase back
that which was lost was paid in full. No other payment will ever
be required.

Think about that last statement for a moment: "No other
payment will ever be required." That means that there is nothing
that you or I could ever do by our own works to assist Jesus in
meeting that ransom demand. The sacrifice of Jesus' body on
the cross, once for all, was completely sufficient in every way to
accomplish paying the steep price of our redemption. Our part
of the redemption process is simply faith. We must completely
rely on and put our full confidence in one thing for our eternal
salvation: the blood of Christ, the ransom price paid to purchase
us back for God.

> **Revelation 5:9-10 -** [9] And they sang a new song: "You are
> worthy to take the scroll and to open its seals, because you
> were slain, and *with your blood you purchased men for God*
> from every tribe and language and people and nation. [10]
> You have made them to be a kingdom and priests to serve
> our God, and they will reign on the earth."

In satisfying God's wrath, we are now called *"the Holy People"*,
"the Redeemed of the Lord", *"sought after"*, *"the City no longer
deserted"* (Isaiah 62:11).

In summary, when we sinned, we exchanged the abundant life we experienced in the garden for the knowledge of good and evil. As a result, we legally became physically and spiritually enslaved to sin and thereby became the object of God's wrath and His righteous judgment. The penalty for this decision was death. Because God is just, He did not cancel this debt; but instead, He sent His own son to pay the debt on our behalf. His blood and His life, which He willingly surrendered on the cross, are the "ransom" price that Christ, our redeemer, paid to buy back and secure our freedom from enslavement to sin and remove from us its punitive consequences.

Through the cross, Jesus made a way for us to be restored to our relationship with God and for us to once again experience the rich, abundant life we were originally created to share with Him before the fall. When He said "It is finished," His work of redemption was complete. This was the purpose of why He came.

> **Matthew 20:28** - ...the Son of Man (that is Christ) did not come to be served, but to serve, and *to give his life as a ransom* for many.

We must understand that it is not Christ's teachings, or doctrine, or moral example through which we are saved; nor is it our religious affiliations, our own moral character, or our own ability to follow God's law. Rather, we are saved solely based on the fact that Jesus satisfied God's wrath and righteous demand for justice by paying the ransom price in full with His own blood, thus removing our sin and its consequences. This was the legal transaction under which we receive all else pertaining to life and godliness in Christ, including, but not limited to, our forgiveness, justification, rebirth or regeneration, righteousness, sanctification, eternal life, and our future inheritance as a saint and child of God. Hebrews 9:22 declares that without the shedding of blood, there is no forgiveness. Faith in the redemptive work of Christ by His shed blood on the cross for our sins, based solely on His grace, or undeserved favor, is what marks the true believer.

At this point, I would like to ask you to personally consider whether or not you have put your reliance upon anything else (i.e., your own good works or moral character, your religious affiliations, your relationships to others, etc.)? If so, I encourage you to make the choice today to quit relying upon your own self-righteousness in the hope that you will someday be "good enough" to inherit eternal life. You cannot fix your broken condition, but there is One who can. Choose instead to place your full confidence in your Redeemer and in the ransom price that He willingly paid on your behalf.

As I have said, the Bible is clear that there is a day coming when God will pour out His wrath on mankind, and we will each stand before Him as the righteous judge (Romans 1:18). If our plea is anything less than God's own grace exhibited through the shed blood of Christ, we are without hope and will be found guilty. In fact, if we are placing our hope in something other than that redemption price, we are claiming that it had something to do with us. In so doing, we are denying the truth that it had everything to do with a willing party who came and paid a horrifically steep price for our freedom from enslavement to sin and death.

So far, we have covered the first three parts of the redemption process:

1. **Something must be lost.** This happened in the garden when we disregarded the abundant life for which we were created by exchanging it for the knowledge of good and evil and a life of independence from God. At that point, we became physically and spiritually enslaved to sin. The judgment for this choice was death in both our body and our spirit and separation from our Creator.

2. **Someone must be willing to pay the price to redeem it.** As we have seen, God the Father had a plan. Jesus agreed to His will.

3. **The ransom price must be paid.** According to the Father's will, Jesus came to Earth and inhabited the body prepared by God for death. He gave His life on the cross as a final guilt offering to satisfy God's wrath against sin. His blood was the ransom price that was paid. This work is finished, and there is no longer a need for any further payment or sacrifice.

The rest of this book will be dedicated to the fourth part of the redemption process: *That which was lost must be returned.*

*"Therefore, if anyone is in Christ, he is a new creation;
the old has gone, the new has come!"*
2 Corinthians 5:17

CHAPTER 3

A ROYAL NEW BIRTH

hroughout New Testament scripture, you will find phrases describing a believer as a person who has been "reborn" or "regenerated," "born-again," "made alive with Christ," as one who is "born of God," and as one who has "crossed over from death to life" (Tit. 3:4-7; Eph. 2:4-5; John 1:10-13, 3:5-8, 5:24). These words are not speaking in future tense, but in past, meaning that this change is something that has already taken place at the point we put our full faith and confidence in the work of Christ on the cross.

What I have found in my own Christian journey is that many believers do not understand the full significance of these gospel truths. If you ask even a seasoned follower of Christ, "How were you born again?" or "What does it mean to be reborn?" many are unable to provide an answer because they have very little understanding of the significance of what God did in them when they believed. Some even perceive these words as being more of a figurative rebirth, or new way of living, rather than a literal change that takes place in us when we believe.

In many church settings, when the gospel is presented, such as during an altar call, typically the speaker will accurately demonstrate the need that we have for salvation and the reality that Jesus is the answer to meet that need. They will then invite the non-believer to exercise their faith in response to Jesus as the source of filling that need. This is not a criticism to that approach; however, unfortunately, discipleship and follow-up is frequently lacking beyond that first moment of decision. As a result, new believers frequently walk away experiencing the freedom and regenerating work of Christ inside of them without truly understanding the full implications of what happened in them when they believed. As the feeling of newness wears off, and the flesh begins to rear its ugly head, they are at a loss for how to deal with fleshly issues victoriously. Many times, these new believers may later even question the validity of their salvation because they are no longer walking in the fresh abundance they experienced at its onset. As a result, over time, our churches have become filled with Christ followers who are not walking in the full reality and truth of God's regenerating work inside of them.

An accurate understanding of the regenerating work of Christ in a believer at salvation is an important key to living the abundant Christian life on this Earth. This understanding helps us identify clearly the issues that we face daily, which pertain to the ongoing battle between our flesh and our spirit. When we can accurately identify the battlefield and our true enemy, we will find greater victory in the battle because we will come to know that God has fully equipped us to be victorious. Often, we simply do not understand the full reality of the arsenal to which we have access.

In Chapter 1, we learned that when Adam and Eve sinned, there were direct consequences to both their body and spirit. They were sold as slaves to sin, and they were changed from God's original design for them. This enslavement to sin and resulting death was passed down from Adam and Eve to the rest of humanity, including us.

When we made the choice to believe, something wonderful changed in this reality. The activation of our faith enabled the ransom price, which had already been paid for our freedom, to be applied to our own personal enslavement. Therefore, if we are in Christ, we are no longer enslaved to sin, which leads to death;

rather, we become a slave to righteousness and to God, which leads to eternal life.

> **Romans 6:17-18** - [17] But thanks be to God that, though you used to be slaves to sin, you wholeheartedly obeyed the form of teaching to which you were entrusted. [18] You have been set free from sin and have become slaves to righteousness.

How did this change take place? The Bible says we were made *new* (2 Cor. 5:17), and we were made *alive* with Christ (Eph. 2:1-10; Colossians 2:13; Romans 5:12-6:23). This transformation is the *good news* of the gospel of Jesus Christ.

Let's take a closer look at what happened to both our spirit and our body at the point of our deliverance.

A New Born Spirit

2 Corinthians 5:17 teaches us that something supernatural and wonderful happened to us when we were saved. Something was newly created. Something "old is gone," and something "new has come." The word "old" in this verse is the Greek word *archaios*, which means "that which has been from the beginning, original, primal."[a] That which is old refers to our old spirit or "sin nature" that was born through Adam under the rule and reign of sin. The word "gone" in this text is *parerchomai* which means "to pass away or perish."[a] This verse is saying that our old fallen spirit no l

exists. It is dead and completely removed from us. It is gone, never to return again! Sometimes, we tend to think of salvation simply as God forgiving us and accepting us as we are into His Kingdom. We think as long as we are trying as hard as we can to keep ourselves on the straight and narrow, or as long as we are *doing our part*, He will continue to do His part and *take care of the rest*. In the end, though we may never say it out loud, we hope that ultimately our best efforts mixed with God's divine grace will be enough to enable us to experience a future glory waiting for us in the resurrection. But 2 Corinthians 5:17 tells us that our old broken spirit is dead *now*. God removed it from our being, and replaced it with a brand new spirit when we believed.

The Greek word for "new" in 2 Corinthians 5:17 is *kainos*, and it means something that is "recently made" or "fresh." The word indicates that the entire substance is of a "brand new kind," or that it is "unprecedented in its nature."[a] This means that the new spirit that God created within us is nothing like what existed before. God did not just make our old spirit better. He didn't just empower it to live righteously sometimes when our own will is strong enough to allow for that, nor did He just cleanse it or forgive it. Instead, He got rid of it, and then He put something completely new and different in its place.

Unlike our old spirit or sin nature, our new spirit did not come through fallen flesh. It was not born through our father and mother, and it cannot be traced back to Adam in our family tree. Rather, it was born directly from God. It was created by the breath or "Spirit" of God, I believe

> *We have been born of imperishable seed originating from God Himself.*

much in the same way that Adam's spirit was originally created by God in the beginning.

The Bible declares that as a new creation in Christ, we have been born of imperishable seed originating from God Himself.

John 1:12-13 - [12] Yet to all who received him, to those who believed in his name, he gave the *right to become children of God*— [13] children *born not of natural descent* (or of blood), nor of human decision or a husband's will, *but born of God.*

1 Peter 1:23 - For you have been born again, *not of perishable seed*, but *of imperishable*, through the living and enduring word of God.

When you hear someone call you a *child of God*, you must realize that this is not figurative language. Those of us who have accepted Christ as our Savior and Lord have literally been reborn directly from God. He is truly our Father, and we are fully His beloved children.

Galatians 4:4-7 - ⁴ But when the time had fully come, God sent his Son, born of a woman, born under law, ⁵ *to redeem* those under law, *that we might receive the full rights of sons.* ⁶ Because you are sons, God sent the Spirit of his Son into our hearts, the Spirit who calls out, "Abba, Father." ⁷ So you are no longer a slave, but a son; and *since you are a son, God has made you also an heir.*

In John 3:5-8, Jesus explains that this spiritual rebirth must take place in order for us to enter the Kingdom of God.

John 3:5-8 - ⁵ Jesus answered, "I tell you the truth, no one can enter the kingdom of God unless he is born of water and the Spirit. ⁶ Flesh gives birth to flesh, but the Spirit gives birth to spirit. ⁷ You should not be surprised at my saying, 'You must be born again.' ⁸ The wind blows wherever it pleases. You hear its sound, but you cannot tell where it comes from or where it is going. So it is with everyone born of the Spirit."

The illustration on the following page demonstrates the literal transformation that occurs in a new believer when they accept Christ as Savior and Lord.

NEW CREATION IN CHRIST
Body Remains Fallen, but Spirit is Made New

What Happened to Our Flesh?

Although our spirit was eternally changed when we first believed in Christ, our body remains in its broken condition. We can tell this by the obvious fact that our body is still the same body today as it was before we were saved. Our body still ages. It remains subject to sickness and disease; and eventually, it is destined to die and return to dust. However, scripture also proclaims that as believers, our spiritual identity (i.e., who we really are) is not in our physical body.

The apostle Peter writes in 2 Peter 1:12-15:

2 Peter 1:12-15 - [12] So I will always remind you of these things, even though you know them and are firmly established in the truth you now have. [13] I think it is right to refresh your memory *as long as I live in the tent of this body,* [14] because I know that *I will soon put it aside,* as our Lord Jesus Christ has made clear to me. [15] And I will make every effort to see that after my departure you will always be able to remember these things.

Here, the apostle Peter describes his body as a "tent," as something that will be "put aside" or discarded. But his identity in this passage is distinctly independent from his own physical body.

The apostle Paul perhaps made the clearest distinctions describing the body as something that is simply material or mortal.

Philippians 1:20-26 - [20] I eagerly expect and hope that I will in no way be ashamed, but will have sufficient courage so that now as always Christ will be exalted in my body, whether by life or by death. [21] For to me, to live is Christ and to die is gain. [22] *If I am to go on living in the body, this will mean fruitful labor for me.* Yet what shall I choose? I do not know! [23] I am torn between the two: I desire to depart and be with Christ, which is better by far; [24] but *it is more necessary for you that I remain in the body.* [25] Convinced of this, I know that I will remain, and I will continue with all of you for your progress and joy in the faith, [26] so that through my being with you again your joy in Christ Jesus will overflow on account of me.

Paul implies that our body is a tool that can be offered to God to accomplish His will and purposes while we live on this earth. In contrast, however, notice that Paul places his own personal identity (i.e., who he really is) in something that is completely and separately distinguishable from his body.

Our physical body can act as both a blessing and a curse to us. In one sense, it holds us back for a season from fully experiencing the completion of Christ's redemptive work in us. It weighs us down. It even fights against us. But on the other hand, there are many who have yet to put their trust in the Messiah. Those who are lost need to be reached with the life-changing reality of Christ's love and grace and the good news of His great plan of redemption. God partners with His people to accomplish His purposes, and even though our body remains weak and fallen, it is the instrument that we have to complete the good works that God has prepared in advance for us to do.

Paul greatly expounds on the marked differences between us as a new spirit and our physical bodies in his second letter to the Corinthians, Chapters 4 & 5. This passage holds great insight into the truth of who we are as a new creation and the continuous struggle we face as we still live within our broken flesh. Let's examine several key verses in this passage:

2 Corinthians 4:6-7 - [6] For God, who said, "Let light shine out of darkness," made his light shine in our hearts to give us the light of the knowledge of the glory of God in the face of Christ. [7] But we have this treasure *in jars of clay* to show that this all-surpassing power is from God and not from us.

The "jars of clay" referenced in this passage refer to our physical bodies. This verse is saying God's light shines in our hearts (which is typically analogous to our human spirit or inner being) giving us the knowledge of the glory of God. However, this great light is housed in jars of clay (our broken physical body) so that God's power can be magnified and so that He may be glorified. Somehow, in God's great plan, the remaining weakness of our flesh serves to remind us, as well as others, that it is God's power at work within us and not our own.

Continuing in Chapter 4, verses 16-18, Paul makes another clear distinction between the nature of our broken flesh and the truth of our new spirit, stating that "outwardly we are wasting away, yet inwardly we are being renewed day by day."

2 Corinthians 4:16-17 - [16] Therefore we do not lose heart. Though *outwardly we are wasting away, yet inwardly we are being renewed day by day.* [17] For our light and momentary troubles are achieving for us an eternal glory that far outweighs them all.

It does not take long to see in the mirror that our body continues to decline as we age, yet this new spirit matures and grows, being renewed daily. There is a clear distinction here that there are two separate and independent parts of us working in direct opposition to one another.

In Chapter 4, verse 18, Paul follows up with an exhortation that our focus should be on what is unseen and eternal.

2 Corinthians 4:18 - So we fix our eyes not on what is seen, but on what is unseen. For what is seen is temporary, but what is unseen is eternal.

If you look at this verse in light of its context, that which is seen and temporary represents our body, while that which is unseen and eternal represents our newly created spirit.

This charge to us is of great importance. Most Christians today spend much more time focusing on the wrongs done in the body, rather than on the righteousness found in our true identity as spirit. Our broken body will be gone someday and this struggle will be over. What will remain is our true identity as a new spirit in Christ. This is not to say that we can allow our bodies to go "unchecked" and to have free license when it comes to sin. On the contrary, the more we understand and accept the truth of what God has already done on the inside, the easier it is for us to dominate the flesh, causing it to lay down in submission to the work of Christ within.

Continuing in 2 Corinthians, Chapter 5, Paul expounds on the struggle we now face as a new born spirit living in a corrupt fallen body. Like Peter, he describes our body as an earthly tent within which our new spirit dwells.

> **2 Corinthians 5:1-6 –** [1] Now we know that if the earthly tent we live in is destroyed *(that is our fleshly physical body*)*, we have a building from God, an eternal house in heaven, not built by human hands *(that is our future eternal body*)*. [2] Meanwhile we groan, longing to be clothed with our heavenly dwelling, [3] because when we are clothed, we will not be found naked. [4] For while we are in this tent, we groan and are burdened, because we do not wish to be unclothed but to be clothed with our heavenly dwelling, so that what is mortal may be swallowed up by life. [5] Now it is God who has made us for this very purpose and has given us the Spirit as a deposit, guaranteeing what is to come. [6] Therefore we are always confident and know that as long as we are at home in the body we are away from the Lord. [7] We live by faith, not by sight.

*Parentheticals are notes from the author.

This is such an amazing passage of scripture because not only does it clearly explain that we are a new spirit living in an "earthly tent" that will one day be destroyed, it also says we will receive a new body which is currently being kept for us in heaven, an eternal house not built by human hands but by God. Notice the difference in the phrase "earthly tent" that is used to describe our earthly body, and the "eternal house" used to describe our new heavenly body. A tent is made to be a temporary dwelling when traveling through a place for a short time, but a house is built to be strong, stable, and enduring. Notice also Paul's remark that when we are clothed with our heavenly dwelling, we will not be found naked. I believe there is a direct correlation here to the account in Genesis when God found Adam and Eve naked, scantily clad in fig leaves, and hiding from Him as a result of their shame (Gen. 2:25).

Our physical body will die someday, returning to the dust from which it came. But just as God has already created us as a new spirit, God has created a brand new body to house us as part of our future inheritance.

This same passage is the context in which we find 2 Corinthians 5:17, the theme verse for this book: *"Therefore if anyone is in Christ, he is a new creation; the old has gone, the new has come!"*

2 Corinthians 5:14-21 - [14] For Christ's love compels us, because we are convinced that one died for all, and therefore all died. [15] And he died for all, that those who live should no longer live for themselves but for him who died for them and was raised again. [16] So from now on we regard no one from a worldly point of view. Though we once regarded Christ in this way, we do so no longer. [17] ***Therefore, if anyone is in Christ, he is a new creation; the old has gone, the new has come!*** [18] All this is from God, who reconciled us to himself through Christ and gave us the ministry of reconciliation: [19] that God was reconciling the world to himself in Christ, not counting men's sins against them. And he has committed to us the message of reconciliation. [20] We are therefore Christ's ambassadors, as though God were making his appeal through us. We implore you on Christ's behalf: Be reconciled to God. [21] God made him who had no sin to be sin for us, so that in him we might become the righteousness of God.

This passage tells us that the 4th part of the redemptive process has already begun inside of us: *That which is lost must be returned.*

> *The 4th part of the redemptive process has already begun inside of us.*

Though we have not yet fully received back all that was lost, we have already been transformed into a beautiful new spirit.

Now, read again 2 Corinthians 5:5:

2 Corinthians 5:5 - Now it is God who has made us for this very purpose and *has given us the Spirit as a deposit, guaranteeing what is to come.*

It might be important to note that the original languages of the Bible did not include punctuation and capitalizations. These were added centuries later by New Testament translators. The Greek word *pneuma* in the New Testament is translated "spirit."[a] The same Greek word is used throughout scripture to refer to our human spirit, as well as to the third person of the trinity – The

"Holy Spirit." It is my belief, based on the context of these two chapters, that the spirit spoken of here is referring to the newly created spirit of a believer, rather than the Holy Spirit. In the immediately preceding text, Paul has been contrasting the differences of our new human spirit with the flesh tent in which it dwells. In context then, it makes sense that he would continue to talk about the same "spirit." This means that the new spirit we received at salvation is given to us as a deposit guaranteeing the rest of the redemptive work that is to come; specifically, the future redemption of our bodies.

After the resurrection, we can be confident that this act of reconciliation will be final and complete. What we need to understand now, however, is that the biggest part of that work has already been accomplished within us when we believed God: that is the exchange of our old spirit for a brand new one. Furthermore, we need to understand that God is not done with us just yet. He has a plan to redeem our broken physical bodies as well. 1 Corinthians 15:35-57 reaffirms this truth:

> **1 Corinthians 15:35-57** - [35] But someone may ask, "How are the dead raised? With what kind of body will they come?" [36] How foolish! What you sow does not come to life unless it dies. [37] When you sow, you do not plant the body that will be, but just a seed, perhaps of wheat or of something else. [38] But God gives it a body as he has determined, and to each kind of seed he gives its own body.

[39] All flesh is not the same: Men have one kind of flesh, animals have another, birds another and fish another. [40] There are also heavenly bodies and there are earthly bodies; but the splendor of the heavenly bodies is one kind, and the splendor of the earthly bodies is another. [41] The sun has one kind of splendor, the moon another and the stars another; and star differs from star in splendor. [42] So will it be with the resurrection of the dead. The body that is sown is perishable, it is raised imperishable; [43] it is sown in dishonor, it is raised in glory; it is sown in weakness, it is raised in power; [44] it is sown a natural body, it is raised a spiritual body. If there is a natural body, there is also a spiritual body. [45] So it is written: "The first man Adam became a living being"; the last Adam, a life-giving spirit. [46] The spiritual did not come first, but the natural, and after that the spiritual. [47] The first man was of the dust of the earth, the second man from heaven. [48] As was the earthly man, so are those who are of the earth; and as is the man from heaven, so also are those who are of heaven. [49] And just as we have **borne the likeness of the earthly man (i.e. Adam), so shall we bear the likeness of the man from heaven (i.e. Christ).** [50] I declare to you, brothers, that flesh and blood cannot inherit the kingdom of God, nor does the perishable inherit the imperishable. [51] Listen, I tell you a mystery: We will not all sleep, but we will all be changed— [52] in a flash, in the twinkling of an eye, at the last trumpet. For the trumpet will sound, the dead will be raised imperishable, and we will be changed. [53] For the perishable must clothe itself with the imperishable, and the mortal with immortality. [54] When the perishable has been clothed with the imperishable, and the mortal with immortality, then the saying that is written will come true: "Death has been swallowed up in victory." [55] "Where, O death, is your victory? Where, O death, is your sting?" [56] The sting of death is sin, and the power of

sin is the law. [57] But thanks be to God! He gives us the victory through our Lord Jesus Christ.

Praise the Almighty God! In that flash, in that twinkling of an eye, God's perfect work of righteousness and redemption will be made perfectly complete in us. We will be restored by God, both in body and spirit, to enjoy a vibrant and abundant life in fellowship with our Creator: free from guilt and shame; free from struggle, sickness, death and pain; completely free from all the lingering effects of sin.

The following illustration reveals the completed work of God that we will experience in our future eternal glory.

ETERNAL RESSURECTED SOUL
Resurrected New Body (Eternal Dwelling)
& Existing New Spirit

John 3:1-2 tells us that God has not made known to us the full reality of what our glorified bodies will be. What we do know, however, is that in our glorified state, we will be *like Him*, and we shall see Him as He is.

> **1 John 3:1-2** - [1] How great is the love the Father has lavished on us, that we should be called children of God! And that is what we are! The reason the world does not know us is that it did not know him. [2] Dear friends, now we are children of God, and what we will be has not yet been made known. But we know that when he appears, (or when it is made known) we shall be **like him**, for we shall see him as he is.

Perhaps, our experience will be far better than the life Adam and Eve experienced in the garden. We will have already made the choice to partake of the Tree of Life, which is Christ, rather than devour the Tree of the Knowledge of Good and Evil. Satan, our accuser, will have received his just judgment from God and will no longer be able to bring his accusations. Because we have received so great a salvation, we will understand the great depths of God's love for us, experiencing relational unity with Him as never before. Whatever the case Saints, the completion of the redeeming work of Christ in our bodies is something to which we can all look forward as we near the end of our time in this life.

For now though, while we are here on this fallen earth, still battling the effects of sin within our fallen flesh, the writer of Hebrews encourages us:

Hebrews 10:19-25 - [19] Therefore, brothers, since we have confidence to enter the Most Holy Place by the blood of Jesus, [20] by a new and living way opened for us through the curtain, that is, his body, [21] and since we have a great priest over the house of God, [22] let us draw near to God with a sincere heart in full assurance of faith, having our hearts sprinkled to cleanse us from a guilty conscience and having our bodies washed with pure water. [23] Let us hold unswervingly to the hope we profess, for he who promised is faithful. [24] And let us consider how we may spur one another on toward love and good deeds. [25] Let us not give up meeting together, as some are in the habit of doing, but let us encourage one another—and all the more as you see the Day approaching.

"In him you were also circumcised, in the putting off of the sinful nature (or the flesh), not with circumcision done by the hands of men but with circumcision done by Christ."
Colossians 2:11-12

CHAPTER 4

MAJESTIC MARKINGS

*I*t is interesting to note that there have been two outward signs in the flesh established by the Word of God that have a direct parallel to the regenerating work of Christ in a believer. The first is found in the Old Testament and is the mark of circumcision, or the outward sign that God gave the Israelites to show their identity and agreement with the covenant God made with their forefather, Abraham. The second is introduced in the New Testament as the believer's baptism.

These two signs are both powerful outward demonstrations of the regenerating work of God performed within our spirit.

Circumcision

In Genesis 15, God spoke to Abraham about a future inheritance that would later belong to him and to his offspring forever. The Bible says that Abraham believed God, and his belief was credited to him as righteousness. Then in Genesis 17, God establishes the practice of circumcision in the flesh as an outward sign of the covenant God made with Abraham and his offspring.

Genesis 17:9-14 - [9] Then God said to Abraham, "As for you, you must keep my covenant, you and your descendants after you for the generations to come. [10] This is my covenant with you and your descendants after you, the covenant you are to keep: Every male among you shall be circumcised. [11] You are to undergo circumcision, and it will be the sign of the covenant between me and you. [12] For the generations to come every male among you who is eight days old must be circumcised, including those born in your household or bought with money from a foreigner—those who are not your offspring. [13] Whether born in your household or bought with your money, they must be circumcised. My covenant in your flesh is to be an everlasting covenant. [14] Any uncircumcised male, who has not been circumcised in the flesh, will be cut off from his people; he has broken my covenant."

Have you ever wondered why circumcision was the sign that God chose to represent this covenant? The word circumcision literally means "a cutting away."[a] The physical circumcision that God required involved an outward cutting away of the flesh, more specifically, the foreskin of the male sex organ. Many people today consider circumcision to be a rather harsh practice inflicted on unsuspecting infants. Was God just seeing how far the Israelites would go to demonstrate their loyalty and obedience, or could circumcision in the flesh be a practice foreshadowing God's future plan of redemption that involved the cutting away and removal of our old dead spirit from our flesh and the surgical replacement of a brand new one?

The Old Testament prophet, Ezekiel, foretold of a time when circumcision would be more than just a physical cutting away. He wrote of a future time when God would "give them an undivided heart and put a new spirit in them," and that He would "remove from them their heart of stone" and replace it with a "heart of flesh." He wrote that God would give them a "new spirit." Ezekiel prophesied that this new spirit, or new heart, would help them to follow God's laws and obey Him (Ezekiel 11:19-20; 36:25-27; Ezekiel 37:1-14).

The New Testament gives us even greater insight into the spiritual circumcision that occurs in a believer. In Romans 2:28-29, Paul sharply contrasts the difference between simply physical or outward circumcision and the circumcision of the heart, which is performed by the Spirit and which is, therefore, pleasing to God.

Romans 2:28-29 - [28] A man is not a Jew if he is only one outwardly, nor is circumcision merely outward and physical. [29] No, a man is a Jew if he is one inwardly; and circumcision is circumcision of the heart, by the Spirit, not by the written code. Such a man's praise is not from men, but from God.

In the time of Paul's letter to the Romans, the Jewish believers of the day were trying to hold Gentile believers to the practice of outward circumcision. Paul contended that what made one of the true household of God was not outward circumcision, but inward circumcision of the heart by the Spirit. Colossians 2:9-15 points out that this circumcision is not done with human hands on physical flesh, rather it is done by Christ himself.

Colossians 2:9-15 - [9] For in Christ all the fullness of the Deity lives in bodily form, [10] and you have been given fullness in Christ, who is the head over every power and authority. [11] In him you were also circumcised, in the putting off of the sinful nature (or the flesh), not with a circumcision done by the hands of men but with the circumcision done by Christ, [12] having been buried with him in baptism and raised with him through your faith in the power of God, who raised him from the dead. [13] When you were dead in your sins and in the uncircumcision of your sinful nature (or your flesh), God made you alive with Christ. He forgave us all our sins, [14] having canceled the written code, with its regulations, that was against us and that stood opposed to us; he took it away, nailing it to the cross. [15] And having disarmed the powers and authorities, he made a public spectacle of them, triumphing over them by the cross.

Scripture is clear that outward circumcision is no longer a requirement for those who come to faith in Christ. However, inward circumcision, or the cutting away of the flesh from our old sin nature and the surgical replacement of our new spirit, is absolutely essential for a believer. This internal circumcision can only be performed employing surgical precision by the nail-scarred hand of Christ Himself in an incredibly significant moment of personal intimacy between us and our Creator occurring the moment of our salvation.

Baptism

The purpose and meaning of the believer's baptism has become the source of many a debate throughout church history. Some teach that the physical act of baptism is what saves a person, asserting that God saves a person in specific response to their obedience through baptism as a demonstration of their faith, rather than salvation being His response to their faith alone. Another teaching on baptism suggests that baptism is simply the

th a person can publicly declare to others that they are

)thers teach baptism as a means to join a particular

)n or church organization; whereas, some teach it as

a symbolic demonstration of a person's belief in Christ's death, burial, and resurrection. Frequently, among all the lines of division on the topic and our own lack of teaching and understanding regarding spiritual regeneration, the deeper significance of the believer's baptism gets overlooked.

It is clear in scripture that circumcision and baptism were both instituted by God as points of obedience that follow faith. However, the Bible is clear that a Jew who simply cuts his flesh, or a person who merely gets wet in water, does not make one a true believer. Those actions, without genuine faith, are of no value. Rather, a person is saved by allowing the ransom price of Christ's shed blood to be applied to his or her own personal enslavement to sin and death by faith, through God's grace alone. It is true that obedience flows directly from true faith or one's belief in God and His Word, and without a doubt, baptism is an important and necessary act of obedience in response to one's belief. However, one who simply focuses on baptism as a point of "obedience," might likely miss the most amazing beauty and truth represented by it.

Water baptism is a beautiful and powerful picture of the spiritual realities that occur in a new believer.

Just as circumcision was an outward demonstration initiated by God to represent spiritual truths pertaining vard transformation, water baptism for the believer takes that demonstration even further. Water baptism is a beautiful and powerful picture of the spiritual realities that occur in a new believer.

> **Romans 6:1-6 –** [1] What shall we say, then? Shall we go on sinning so that grace may increase? [2] By no means! We died to sin; how can we live in it any longer? [3] Or don't you know that all of us who were baptized into Christ Jesus were *baptized into his death*? [4] We were therefore buried *with him* through baptism into death in order that, *just as* Christ was raised from the dead through the glory of the Father, *we too may live a new life.* [5] If we have been *united with him* like this in his death, we will certainly also be *united with him* in his resurrection. [6] For we know that our old self was *crucified with him* so that the body of sin might be done away with, that we should no longer be slaves to sin.

There is something intensely personal and intimate in the fellowship that we share with Christ through water baptism. We were crucified with Him. We have been buried with Him. We are raised with Him, and we are united with Him. Baptism is the outward demonstration of this inward reality. The profound unity that we are enabled to share with Jesus in this very special way is truly sweet, glorious, and very real.

As we go through the symbolic process of burying that old sin nature through baptism, we begin to understand and accept that we are no longer identified with it. Baptism is a declaration to God, to ourselves, to the world, and to the powers of hell, that we have been eternally changed by the redeeming power of the blood of Jesus Christ. It attests to the fact that our old sin nature is dead, buried, and forever removed from our being. It loudly proclaims that we have become "like Him" in His death, burial, and resurrection. It testifies of the future glory awaiting us, and it affirms that we are a born-again child of the Most High God.

When we bury something, we don't typically go dig it up again to re-examine it. We understand it is gone, and the process of burial helps us to recognize that fact and let it go. Can you imagine if we dug up our dead every time we began to miss them? But sometimes, even after baptism, we try to do this very thing with our old dead spirit. We choose to look back and find our personal identity in our old sin nature. Each time we do that, it is as if we go digging up a dead rotting corpse, tie ourselves to it, and then drag it around with us everywhere we go. We must learn to let go of that dead thing.

"I do not understand what I do. For what I want to do
I do not do, but what I hate I do."
Romans 7:15

CHAPTER 5

WHO WILL SAVE ME ... FROM THIS BODY?

⎯⎯⎯⎯⎯⎯⎯⎯⎯⎯⎯❧⎯⎯⎯⎯⎯⎯⎯⎯⎯⎯⎯

*B*y now, you may be asking, "If I am a New Creation, why don't I feel like it all the time? Why do I still struggle with sin?" First, it might help you to know that the apostle Paul shared this same struggle.

Romans 7:14-15 - ¹⁴ We know that the law is spiritual; but I am unspiritual, sold as a slave to sin. ¹⁵ I do not understand what I do. For what I want to do I do not do, but what I hate I do.

The Greek word for "want" in this passage is *etheleo* which means "to will, to have in mind, to intend; to be resolved or determined, to purpose; to desire, to wish; to love; to like to do a thing, be fond of doing; to take delight in or have pleasure."[a] In other words, the things that I *will myself, or have in mind, or intend to do; those things I am resolved to do or determined or purposed to do,* ... I do not do. Instead, however, I do those things that I hate or detest to do. Does this sound familiar?

This passage provides excellent insight into several key truths we need to understand concerning the realities of our true identity as spirit and the corrupt fallen nature of our broken flesh.

1. As spirit, we love God's law and want to do what is right.

2. The nature of our flesh is against God's law and does not want to do what is right.

3. As spirit, we hate sin and do not want to do what is wrong.

4. The nature of our flesh remains fallen under the effects of sin and is bent toward doing what is evil.

Even though this may sound a little bit like spiritual schizophrenia, Paul was contrasting two different realities here: the reality of his true identity as spirit and the reality of his broken flesh. Paul felt the same conflict with sin that you and I do today.

Understanding these four basic statements of truth about our fallen flesh and our new spirit can go a long way in helping us identify what is dominating our lives at any given moment. It is important for us to know that as a new spirit, who has been born

71

of God, we were perfectly created to love what God loves and hate what God hates. However, the law that is at work in our flesh constantly tries to make us a prisoner or a slave again to sin.

Before moving forward, let's take a moment to define what the flesh actually is.

What is our flesh?

At its root, the flesh can most easily be defined as the tent in which we live. We *are* a spirit. We live *in* a body of flesh.

> We *are* a spirit. We live *in* a body of flesh.

In the New Testament, the Greek words translated as "flesh" are *sarx*, *sarkinos* and *sarkikos*. Each of these words describes things pertaining to the body that are of earthly or perishable material.[a] Our flesh is the part of us that was formed out of dust in the Garden of Eden and the part of us that will return to dust when we die. At a minimum, our flesh includes the substance that makes up our physical bodies, such as our bones, tissues, and vital organs.

It is important to note that the most significant and most influential vital organ of our body is the human brain. Our brain is a powerfully complex, yet necessary, part of our fallen flesh. Scientists continue to uncover new mysteries about the various roles and functions of the grey matter that occupies the space between our ears. Through scientific research, we have learned that the brain houses the bodily functions of memory, as well as various aspects of emotion, cognitive reasoning, and personality. One way to recognize that these vital functions are produced, at least in part, through our human brain is to examine people who have experienced trauma or physical injury to the brain such as through a stroke or an accident. Frequently, we see that trauma to the brain can have an adverse effect to the neurological functions of memory, cognitive reasoning, emotion, and/or personality. In addition to trauma, these essential neurological functions of the brain can also be negatively influenced by hormonal and chemical imbalances, or impeded by outside substances introduced into the body such as drugs and alcohol.

Additionally, we have learned in recent years that habits are formed in the brain. Neuro-scientific research has shown that habitual thinking patterns or actions, whether positive or negative, can actually create neurological signatures or grooves in the brain that carry the patterns of thought associated with a particular habit. When presented with the right scenario for the habit to exert itself, the brain activates the neurons that carry the thought patterns of the particular habit and assists the rest of the body in carrying it out. Recent studies have shown that you can overcome bad habits by creating new grooves in the brain with different thinking patterns over time.[b]

This natural understanding of our human physiology, particularly, the role and functions of the brain, aids us in discovering how our fallen flesh might still present us with problems submitting to its new tenant. The Bible tells us that the flesh has its own mind and appetite, separate and independent from that of our new spirit. One possible reason for this could be that before we were saved, the same brain that we now have communicating with our new spirit, previously received its instruction and influence from our old spirit or sin nature. Before Christ, our brain had time for habits to form, negative thinking patterns to evolve, and memories associated with sin to find a foothold. These habits, thinking patterns, and memories are still present in our brain even after we become a newly created spirit in Christ.

Though our flesh retains patterns, habits, and appetites toward sin, we must recognize that our spiritual identity does not come from the activities of the flesh. The DNA of our newly created spirit is altogether different. In summing up his own struggle with the flesh, Paul makes this very bold statement:

Romans 7:17 - As it is, it is no longer I myself who do it, but it is sin living in me.

Paul clearly understood that the sin he faced as a believer was not who he was before God, rather it was something that was left over as a residual, present only within the temporary dwelling of his still fallen flesh. He knew with confidence that his true spiritual identity lay only in the reality of him being a newly created spirit in Christ Jesus.

If this was true for Paul, then it should also be true for you and me. So, I ask this question. If you are a believer in Christ, can you agree with Paul's statement concerning your own sin? Can you say with confidence as Paul did, "When I sin, it is no longer I who sins; but, it is sin living in me that does it?" For some of us, making such a bold statement baffles the mind and shakes the very core of all our religious upbringing. However, only when we can agree with the Word of God concerning the true source of our struggle against sin, will we ever be effective in dealing with it.

In Verse 18, Paul expounds:

Romans 7:18-20 - [18] I know that *nothing good lives in me,* that is, in my sinful nature (or flesh). For I have the desire to do what is good, but I cannot carry it out. [19] For what I do is not the good I want to do; no, the evil I do not want to do—this I keep on doing. [20] Now if I do what I do not want to do, it is no longer I who do it, but it is sin living in me that does it.

75

This statement is extremely significant to our walk while in this body. When we are convinced that literally ***nothing*** good can come from our broken flesh, we quit trying to *dress it up,* and we quit trying to live out of it in some way

> *Nothing* good
> can come
> from our
> broken flesh.

that would please God. Many of us, even after becoming a new creation in Christ, find ourselves trying very hard to clean up the outside as best we can. We do good deeds in the flesh. We attempt to force our flesh to conform to some standard of what we think righteousness looks like from the outside. Then, we take that before our Holy God, hoping that He might find some pleasure or joy in our offering; yet, when we believe the Word of God that says truly ***nothing*** good can come from our flesh, we begin to understand the vital importance of laying the flesh down completely. Then, instead of presenting rotten, putrid flesh as our offering to God, we present ourselves to Him as the new creation that He has graciously made us to be. Let's take a quick look at a passage in Philippians 3 pertaining to this very thing:

> **Philippians 3:3-11** - [3] For it is we who are the circumcision, we who worship by the Spirit of God, who glory in Christ Jesus, and who put no confidence in the flesh— [4] though I myself have reasons for such confidence. If anyone else thinks he has reasons to put confidence in the flesh, I have more: [5] circumcised on the eighth day, of

the people of Israel, of the tribe of Benjamin, a Hebrew of Hebrews; in regard to the law, a Pharisee; [6] as for zeal, persecuting the church; as for legalistic righteousness, faultless. [7] But whatever was to my profit I now consider loss for the sake of Christ. [8] What is more, I consider everything a loss compared to the surpassing greatness of knowing Christ Jesus my Lord, for whose sake I have lost all things. I consider them rubbish, that I may gain Christ [9] and be found in him, ***not having a righteousness of my own that comes from the law, but that which is through faith in Christ***—the righteousness that comes from God and is by faith. [10] I want to know Christ and the power of his resurrection and the fellowship of sharing in his sufferings, becoming like him in his death, [11] and so, somehow, to attain to the resurrection from the dead.

We always face a choice of two options in which we can place our confidence before God. The first option is to rely upon our own righteousness, or our own perceived ability through fallen flesh to please God. The other option is to rely completely upon God's free gift of righteousness, which has been imparted to us as a new spiritual being by faith. There is no provision to choose "C - All of the above." As believers, we often live as if the goal of our Christian walk is to perfect the fallen flesh. We think that the better we are able to do that, the better we look and, therefore, the more pleasing we are to God. When we feel successful in our attempts, we tend to walk in pretentious, religious pride. When we feel unsuccessful in our attempts, we tend to hide from

God and retreat into desperation and despair. We are sabotaging ourselves when we do this because, in either case, we are looking for our reward to come from fallen flesh that has "nothing good" in it to offer to God. Our fallen flesh has never pleased God, and it never will. We must stop trying to live as if it does. The deeds generated out of the flesh are of no value (wood, hay and stubble); however, those works spawned by the spirit will stand the test of fire on the Day of Judgment and will be proven as gold, silver, and precious stones (1 Corinthians 3:10-15).

Paul then concludes with:

Romans 7:21-24 - [21] So I find this law at work: When I want to do good, evil is right there with me. [22] For in my inner being I delight in God's law; - [23] but I see another law at work in the members of my body, waging war against the law of my mind and making me a prisoner of the law of sin at work within my members. [24] What a wretched man I am! Who will rescue me from this body of death?

As long as we live in this fallen flesh tent, we will constantly have the battle between the "want to," or "desire," of our new spirit and the residing sin still present within our broken flesh, which fights constantly against that desire.

Even in his writing, Paul screams out what we all want to scream out ... "What a wretched man I am! Who will rescue me from *this body* of death?" It is very frustrating to have these two things in such direct opposition to each other and to know that while we live in this body, we will have an ever present struggle with sin. The more we understand the source of this struggle, however, the more we, like Paul, will also truly begin to detest our flesh, realizing that it is holding us back from doing what we truly want to do. Instead of relishing in it, trying to *dress it up* as our offering to God, we will understand even more the benefit of us learning to put it to death by the spirit, so that we might effectively walk as the glorious new creation that God has already designed us to be.

I love Paul's answer to his own question as he reminds us of the inheritance of our future glorified bodies: "Thank you God, it is because of Jesus our Lord that I will be rescued from it." (paraphrase) – Then, however, he quickly reminds us again of the truth we must all face for now until that day of rescue comes:

> **Romans 7:25b** - So then, I myself in my mind am a slave to God's law, but in the sinful nature *(flesh)* a slave to the law of sin.

It is imperative to understand that the real "you" lies in your true identity as spirit, not in the fallen flesh tent in which you live. We do not have two natures. We have one nature and that nature is found in Christ. Our flesh often deceives us into believing that what we see through it is our true identity. It is not. The Bible says that when you fail to live up to the righteous standard that is already written on your heart and mind as a new spirit, it is the sin that is at work in your flesh causing you to live that way. It is not you. We must remember that our flesh, or body, is destined to die and return to dust. Our identity does not come from that which is temporary. It comes from that which is eternal, and it is solely recognized as that glorious New Creation that God made us on the day of our salvation.

In this life, we need to understand that we will never be 100% victorious over the sin of our flesh because our flesh is still fallen, and it still maintains its relationship as a slave to sin. Amazingly, contrary to popular teaching, that is not even our goal as a believer. Complete victory over the flesh will only come once our fallen flesh dies and returns to dust, when God presents each of us with a new glorified body at the resurrection - "an eternal house in the heavens, not built by human hands" (2 Cor. 5:1). Does this mean that we allow the flesh to control and dominate our activity in this life? Absolutely not! God has, through His Word, provided us with plenty of instructions about how to effectively deal with the issue of sin in the flesh. We will be taking some time to look at this instruction in detail in a later chapter; however, before doing so, we first need to discover the astounding beauty that God has crafted within each of us as a born again new spirit in Christ.

"God made him who had no sin to be sin for us, so that in him we might become the righteousness of God."
2 Corinthians 5:21

CHAPTER 6

DISCOVERING TRUE BEAUTY

Few of us have a clear picture of who we really are as a new creation in Christ; however, understanding what the Bible says about our new spirit is imperative to learning how to walk in the fullness of all that God has created us to be. This chapter is dedicated to uncovering several key foundational points, specifically pertaining to our new spirit's relationship to righteousness, sin, and the law. There are four major mysteries that we will unlock as we begin to delve deeper into discovering the true beauty of God's workmanship inside of us.

As a New Spirit in Christ:

1. We are created in the image of God.

2. We are endowed with God's own righteousness and holiness.

3. We are not under law.

4. We cannot sin.

Let's begin with the first statement:

As a new spirit, we are created in the image of God.

Remember, Genesis 1:27 records that when Adam and Eve were originally created, they were created in the image or likeness of God. In this same chapter, we find that God proclaimed that everything He had made was very good; yet, for those born after Adam, something significant changed. Rather than being born bearing the righteous and holy image of God, we were born bearing the image of the fallen man, Adam. This significant truth is first encountered in the genealogical account of Adam's offspring in Genesis 5:1-3:

> **Genesis 5:1-3** - [1] This is the written account of Adam's line. When God created man, he made him *in the likeness of God*. [2] He created them male and female and blessed them. And when they were created, he called them "man." [3] When Adam had lived 130 years, he had *a son in his own likeness, in his own image*; and he named him Seth.

Let's take a closer look at what our redeeming Messiah did about this problem. Romans 8:3 tells us that God sent his own son *in the likeness* of sinful man to be a sin offering, *so that* the righteous requirements of the law could be *fully* met in us who live according to the spirit.

> **Romans 8:3-4** – ³ For what the law was powerless to do in that it was weakened by the sinful nature ^(or flesh), God did by sending his own Son *in the likeness* of sinful man to be a sin offering. And so he condemned sin in sinful man, ⁴ in order that the righteous requirements of the law might be fully met in us, who do not live according to the sinful nature but according to the Spirit.

We already have learned in Chapter 3 that our resurrected body will bear the likeness of God in the resurrection.

> **1 Corinthians 15:47-49** - ⁴⁷ The first man was of the dust of the earth, the second man from heaven. ⁴⁸ As was the earthly man, so are those who are of the earth; and as is the man from heaven, so also are those who are of heaven. ⁴⁹ And just as we **have borne the likeness of the earthly man, so shall we bear the likeness of the man from heaven.**

Remember, this passage was part of Paul's response to the question, "How are the dead raised, with what kind of *body* will they come?" What about our new spirit? To answer this question, we need to take a closer look at Ephesians 4:22-24:

Ephesians 4:22-24 - [22] You were taught, with regard to your former way of life, to put off your old self, which is being corrupted by its deceitful desires; [23] to be made new in the attitude of your minds; [24] and to put on the new self, ***created to be like God in true righteousness and holiness.***

The Greek literally says our new self, or spirit, was "created *after the likeness* of God." Notice the incredible magnitude of God's redeeming power to reclaim for us that which we had lost in the garden as a result of our rebellion. At the moment of our faith in Christ, that instant when we became a born-again new creation in Christ, we were once again molded by the Almighty hand of God to be a beautiful reflection of His glorious likeness.

Now, let's take a look at specifically how we reflect the image of God.

As a new spirit, we are endowed with God's own righteousness and holiness.

Ephesians 4:24 says our new self was created to be like God (or in his image) in *"true righteousness and holiness."* That word *true* literally means "of the truth; in fact, reality, or certainty."[a] When we became a new creation in Christ Jesus, it is a matter of fact and certainty that our new spirit was endowed with God's own attributes of righteousness and holiness.

In a future chapter, we will discover what it means to *put on* the new self and *take off* the old; however first, we need to grab hold of this one incredible point: our new spirit is created to be *like God* in true righteousness and holiness. To get the full magnitude of this statement, we need to understand some vital points concerning righteousness.

First, the imputation of God's own righteousness is paramount to the gospel of Jesus Christ. Romans 1:17 tells us that in the gospel, or good news of Jesus Christ, a righteousness *from God* is revealed, a righteousness that is by faith from first to last (see also Romans 3:21-26). Notice the righteousness, spoken about in the gospel, does not come from us. It has nothing to do with our own aptitude or ability to follow God's laws perfectly. Rather, the righteousness referred to in the gospel originates from God Himself and is imparted to us when, through faith, we become a born-again child of a righteous and holy God.

When we are born from something, we take on the characteristics of that from which we are born. In this case, our new spirit is born directly from God and has been supernaturally imparted with the most wonderful qualities of His own righteousness and holiness. Let me ask you a question. If God is imparting His own righteousness and holiness to you, as a new spirit, would He give you anything less than perfect and pure righteousness? Would that righteousness be limited in any way? Consider the fact that God put His own name on the label.

Second, though we tend to think of righteousness as subjective and relative, we need to understand that God has only one perfect standard of righteousness. That standard is His own absolute perfection. That standard never changes because God never changes. His standard of righteousness was the same before man sinned in the garden, it was the same between the time of Adam and the law, it was the same after the law was given to Moses, and it is the exact same today. To God, righteousness is not some loose, changing, or obscure term that cannot be measured or that is comparatively or relatively measured one against another. Rather, righteousness is an absolute, non-subjective, ideal truth that has a fixed meaning, and it is something that God can absolutely qualitatively and quantitatively measure. For God though, that absolute is all or nothing. There is no in between. We either are righteous or we aren't; so, thank God, it is not up to us to meet that standard. If it were, we would desperately be without hope. What He requires of us is to believe in the ransom price that He paid on our behalf and in the One who paid it; then, through that faith, God makes us brand new on the inside. With that newness, comes the free gift of His own perfect righteousness. This is the

> *God has only one perfect standard of righteousness. That standard is His own absolute perfection.*

gospel or good news of Jesus Christ. If we miss this truth, we have missed understanding the very core of the gospel itself.

Now, look again at 2 Corinthians 5:17-21:

2 Corinthians 5:17-21 - [17] *Therefore, if anyone is in Christ, he is a new creation; the old has gone, the new has come!* [18] All this is from God, who reconciled us to himself through Christ and gave us the ministry of reconciliation: [19] that God was reconciling the world to himself in Christ, not counting men's sins against them. And he has committed to us the message of reconciliation. [20] We are therefore Christ's ambassadors, as though God were making his appeal through us. We implore you on Christ's behalf: Be reconciled to God. [21] God made him who had no sin to be sin for us, *so that in him we might become the righteousness of God.*

The Greek word for reconcile is *katallasso* which means "to change, or exchange."[a] Notice specifically, verse 21, *"God made him who had no sin to be sin for us, so that in him, we might become the righteousness of God."* God's plan of redemption has always been that we be returned to once again fully reflect God's image of true righteousness and holiness. Sometimes, however, we tend to think that God has just wiped our slate clean by giving us a "do over." We may understand that we, through Christ, have been forgiven of our past sin or that we have been made in right standing with God. All of these statements are absolutely true; however, His gift of righteousness goes deeper than this. The gospel declares that the way in which God met His own demand for perfect righteousness is by *becoming sin* so that we could *become His righteousness*, specifically that we would become <u>the</u> righteousness of God. The way He did this is through the process of reconciliation and redemption. He crucified our dead broken spirit and raised us to life with Him as a brand new spirit perfectly created to be like Him in true righteousness and holiness.

As a new spirit, we are not under law.

This next point is another wonderful statement of fact concerning who we are as a new spirit. I am going to take time to carefully develop it because I understand the "shock" factor and the "Yes, but..." questions that arise when we consider the full implications of this statement.

Before we look at why we are not under law anymore, we need to first understand some foundational principles concerning the law: What is the law really? Why was it given to us? What consequence does it have concerning our walk with God?

Simply put, the law is God's perfect standard of righteousness revealed to man. Galatians 3:24 tells us that the law was "put in charge to lead us to Christ." Romans 3:20 tells us exactly how this occurs: "through the law, we become conscious of sin." The law was given for the expressed purpose of revealing God's righteous standard and imparting to us a conscious awareness of our sin. Romans 7:13 tells us that the law helped us to recognize sin as sin so that, *through the commandment, sin might become utterly sinful.* Romans 5:20-21 further states that the law was added so that the "trespass might increase;" yet, where sin increased, God's grace increased all the more.

When God sends His word, it accomplishes exactly what He wants it to accomplish. We know that the law has in fact both made us conscious of our sin and achieved its goal of leading us to Christ. The law, however, has had other powerful consequences as well.

To understand these consequences, we must once again take the journey back to our genesis before the fall. In the garden, there was one tree that Adam and Eve were told to avoid: the Tree of the Knowledge of Good and Evil. When they ate of this particular tree, there were two very important direct consequences for their choice. First, they gained exactly what the name of the tree suggests, which is a literal knowledge of good and evil. Second, they became physically and spiritually enslaved to sin. We already know the ultimate end result for gaining this knowledge of good and evil and becoming enslaved to sin is death; however, what other effects did these consequences have on our ability to live up to God's standard of righteousness after the fall.

Our enslavement to sin meant that we had a new "master" or "lord" dominating us. Sin was continuously present within us seeking every opportunity to express itself as the one in control. Romans 6:20 tells us that "when we were slaves to sin, we were free from the control of righteousness." Sin, therefore, was the governing force in both our body and spirit which were both fallen and altered from God's original design. Because of this, we had no power to ever meet the perfect righteous standard God requires.

The knowledge of good and evil, paired with sin being in charge as our master made a very lethal combination in fallen man. Let me explain this further.

Before the written law was given through Moses, we were not fully aware of the extent of our sin or God's view of it, nor were we aware of the severe consequences for it. However, remember my previous statement: God's righteous standard of perfection never changes. There is only one standard, and we were already failing to perfectly live up to it because sin within us was seizing every opportunity it could find to follow its own evil desires. James 2:10 says that "whoever keeps the whole law and yet stumbles in just one point, is guilty of breaking all of it." Therefore, even a seemingly *good person* would not meet this righteous standard in God's eyes.

Romans 5:13 says that "sin is not taken into account when there is no law." God, therefore, gave us the written law, through Moses, as a way to reveal His perfect standard of righteousness, as well as to make us aware of how much we were missing the mark. However, as the law was given, or as God's righteous standard was revealed, our trespass increased. Why? First of all, with more knowledge of the law, came more accountability for sin. Romans 5:20-21 explains that this was actually an intended result of the law.

> **Romans 5:20-21** - [20] The law was added so that the trespass might increase. But where sin increased, grace increased all the more, [21] so that, just as sin reigned in death, so also grace might reign through righteousness to bring eternal life through Jesus Christ our Lord.

Furthermore, Romans 7:5 tells us that "when we were controlled by the sinful nature, the sinful passions aroused by the law were at work in our bodies, so that we bore fruit for death." The word "aroused by" in the Greek is *deeah*. It is a primary preposition denoting the direct channel of an act. It literally means "by means of, through, the ground or reason by which something is or is not done."[a] The law was the channel

The law is the channel through which sinful passions are aroused.

through which sinful passions already present within our broken body were awoken.

Consider the record of Adam and Eve's lure into disobedience. The first thing the serpent did was to point out the only command that had been given to Adam and Eve from God. He said to the woman, "Did God really say, 'You must not eat from any tree in the garden?'" (Genesis 3:1) He first brought the command to the forefront of her mind. Then, he brought into question the nature of God's character and His best intentions toward her saying, "You will not die, for God knows that when you eat of it, your eyes will be opened, and you will be like God, knowing good and evil." In a way this was true. When Adam and Eve ate from the tree of the Knowledge of Good and Evil, they became aware of God's righteous moral law. However, because sin was their new master, as a result of their disobedience, this knowledge actually incited them again and again to further sin. The knowledge of law, coupled with the occupancy of sin as our master, actually puts within us the overwhelming desire to break the command.

The following diagram illustrates this point:

TRUTH OF OUR OLD NATURE BEFORE CHRIST

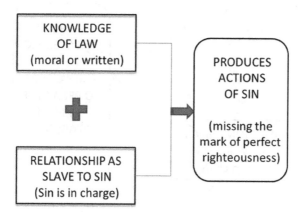

Conversely, without that knowledge and/or without sin being our master, the desire to break the command is absent.

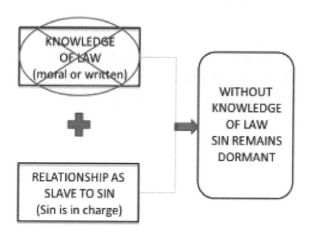

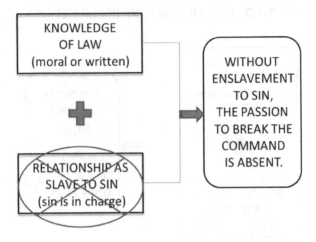

The same is true for the written law. Because sin is present within us due to the fall, the law actually causes an arousal of that sin. Let's take a look at the practical example Paul gives us of this truth, found in Romans 7:7:

> **Romans 7:7** - What shall we say, then? Is the law sin? Certainly not! Indeed I would not have known what sin was except through the law. For I would not have known what coveting really was if the law had not said, "Do not covet."

Remember in verse 5, Paul has just made the statement that the law is the channel through which sinful passions are aroused. Now he anticipates their next question: "So is the law sin?" He uses an example from one of the Ten Commandments: "Thou shalt not covet." Following through with this same example, what we need to understand is that coveting was always against God's perfect righteous standard, regardless of whether or not we fully understood that fact. Even though, at one time, we were unaware of the law that says "Thou shalt not covet," we still had the inclination and disposition within our fallen state to covet and thereby become the deserving objects of God's wrath. Therefore, in love, God revealed to us His perfect law about coveting, enabling us to understand that, in coveting, we were missing the mark of His perfect righteousness. The written revelation of the law, however, produced a startling consequence:

> **Romans 7:8** - But sin, seizing the opportunity afforded by the commandment, produced in me every kind of covetous desire. For apart from law, sin is dead.

Paul says by gaining the knowledge of the commandment, "Thou shalt not covet," it produced within him every kind of covetous desire. Why would simply gaining knowledge about this command have such a powerful result? Remember, we were sold as slaves to sin. If sin is your master, or the one in control, then when it learns the commandment that reveals God's perfect standard of righteousness, "Thou shalt not covet," it innately and instinctively gives you the order to walk completely in the opposite direction of what you know to be righteous.

Paul continues this passage, taking us deeper into understanding how the knowledge of law and the indwelling nature of sin present within us results in death.

> **Romans 7:9-12 -** [9] Once I was alive apart from law; but when the commandment came, sin sprang to life and I died. [10] I found that the very commandment that was intended to bring life actually brought death. [11] For sin, seizing the opportunity afforded by the commandment, deceived me, and through the commandment put me to death. [12] So then, the law is holy, and the commandment is holy, righteous and good.

The only time that Paul would have once been "alive apart from the law" is when he was a child before the age of accountability, that is before his personal awareness of the commandment. Look what happened when the commandment came: "Sin sprang to life." Notice the word "life" here is in direct contrast with his previous statement in verse 8, "for apart from law, sin is *dead*." The colorful expression of this verse demonstrates how when sin is your master, it lies dormant waiting for an opportunity. It might help to think of sin like a lioness on the prowl, crouching down, and lying low until the perfect opportunity arises. Likewise, the master "sin" lays dormant waiting for the first opportunity to "spring to life." The opportunity comes when sin is presented with the commandment or the law. The commandment itself arouses or awakens the evil passions that are already present within us.

Then sin, as the "master" seizing the opportunity, "springs to life" and "deceives" us.

Merriam Webster's collegiate dictionary defines the term *deceive* as "to cause to accept as true or valid what is false or invalid; to give a false impression; to lead astray or frustrate by underhandedness." It states that to deceive implies "imposing a false idea or belief that causes ignorance, bewilderment, or helplessness." It means "to mislead, delude which implies deceiving so thoroughly as to obscure the truth." It means "to beguile, which stresses the use of charm and persuasion in deceiving."[c] Notice the source of this deception comes from sin that is present within us. The result is death.

James 1:13-15 affirms this point:

James 1:13-15 - [13] When tempted, no one should say, "God is tempting me." For God cannot be tempted by evil, nor does he tempt anyone; [14] but each one is tempted when, *by his own evil desire*, he is dragged away and enticed. [15] Then, after desire has conceived, it gives birth to sin; and sin, when it is full-grown, gives birth to death.

The Greek words for "dragged away" and "enticed" are *exelko* and *deleazo*, respectively, which are hunting terms meaning "to draw out" or "to be lured from a hiding place" or "seduced" by bait.[a] Notice that temptation happens by "our own evil desire." More specifically, it is the sin presently residing within us due to our fallen state. The Greek word for "conceived" in verse 15 is *syllambanomai*, which literally means "to seize, catch or capture."[a] This verse is saying that we are tempted when the sin present within us is drawn out and baited. Then once that sin has been seized or captured, it produces the actions associated with sin. That sin, becoming full grown, brings forth or produces death. Interestingly, the way that sin is drawn out and baited most often comes from its awareness of the commandment.

Let me give you a couple of very simple and practical examples of how this progression still happens within our fallen flesh. If you were to give your flesh the command, "Don't eat pizza for the next 2 weeks," most likely pizza is the only thing your body will crave for the next two weeks. Have you ever seen a sign that says, "Wet paint. Don't touch." What did you do?

Both of these passages clearly demonstrate the chronological sequence of how residing sin, coupled with the law, leads to the judgment of death:

1. First we are alive.
2. Then the command comes.
3. Sin, living dormant within us, is awoken by the command and springs to life.
4. Once sin is born, the end result is death.

We need to understand, however, that the law was never intended to bring righteousness. The writer of Hebrews tells us that the law was only a shadow of the good things that are coming, not the realities themselves. For this reason, it could never make perfect those who draw near to worship (Hebrews 10:1).

Now that we understand what the law is and the purpose and consequences of it, let's go back to the basic truth regarding the nature of our true identity as a new spirit: As a new spirit, we are not under law.

First of all, let's biblically establish the fact that as a new creation in Christ, we are no longer under the law. As previously stated, the law had a specific purpose to lead us to Christ by revealing to us that we were missing God's perfect standard of righteousness; however, in Galatians 3:25, Paul testifies "now that faith has come, we are no longer under the supervision of the law."

Now that faith has come, we are no longer under the supervision of the law. (Galatians 3:25)

Why would this be true? Don't we still need to know God's righteous standards and keep them? Absolutely! But remember the first two points we learned in this chapter about our new spiritual identity. We were created in God's own image and imparted with God's own righteousness and holiness. Therefore, as a new creation, the righteous requirements of the law of God are already "fully met" in us who do not living according to the sinful nature of our flesh, but according to the spirit (Romans 8:4).

The prophet Jeremiah spoke of a time when God's law would be written on our hearts:

> **Jeremiah 31:33** – "This is the covenant I will make with the house of Israel after that time," declares the LORD. "I will put my law in their minds and write it on their hearts. I will be their God, and they will be my people."

Romans 7:22 tells us that as a new spirit in Christ, we "delight in God's law." So we don't need to be afraid of our new spirit breaking the command or somehow being thwarted from living out the one absolute standard God has for righteousness.

As part of the redemption process, Galatians 3:13 tells us that "Christ redeemed us from the curse of the law, by becoming a curse for us." Paul explains in Romans 7:1, that the "law has authority over a man only as long as he lives." The law was necessary to lead our old spirit to Christ's work on the cross. But now that our old spirit is dead, what need would the law serve for our new spirit that is already created to be perfectly righteous? Going further, let's take a look at the next part of chapter 7:

> **Romans 7:4-6** - ⁴ So, my brothers, you also died to the law through the body of Christ, that you might belong to another, to him who was raised from the dead, in order that we might bear fruit to God. ⁵ For when we were controlled by the sinful nature, the sinful passions aroused by the law were at work in our bodies, so that we bore fruit for death. ⁶ But now, by dying to what once bound

us, we have been released from the law so that we serve in the new way of the Spirit, and not in the old way of the written code.

As a believer, we should see a marked difference in the way the fruit of righteousness is produced through our lives. Rather than our old way, before Christ, of trying by ourselves to live up to God's righteous standards on our own, now, in Christ, we have the fruit of God's own pure righteousness perfectly enabled to flow through us. In contrast, when we are not walking in the truth of our new spiritual identity, we quickly encounter that age old struggle between our knowledge of the law and the sin present within our still broken flesh that so desperately desires to entrap us.

Romans 4:15 tells us that the law brings wrath. But where there is no law, there is no transgression or sin. This brings me to the last point.

Our new spirit cannot sin.

Because of the redeeming work of Christ, sin has been dealt with in sinful man. Paul makes a wonderful statement found in Romans 6:14:

> **Romans 6:14** - Sin shall not be your master, because you are not under law, but under grace.

We've already pointed out the fact that we are not under law;

however, this verse also clearly states that sin is no longer our master. Though we were once enslaved to sin in our old nature, our new spirit belongs to God. Let's go back to Romans, chapter 6:

> **Romans 6:17-18** - [17] But thanks be to God that, though you used to be slaves to sin, you wholeheartedly obeyed the form of teaching to which you were entrusted. [18] You have been set free from sin and have become slaves to righteousness.

When presented with the question, "Shall we go on sinning that grace may abound," Paul responds in Romans 6:2 that "We died to sin, how can we live in it any longer?" Then in verses 6 and 7 of that same chapter, he expounds, "For we know that our old self was crucified with Him so that the *body of sin* might be done away with, that we should no longer be slaves to sin—because anyone who has died has been freed from sin."

1 John 3:5 also tells us that in Christ, there is no sin.

> **1 John 3:4-5** - [4] Everyone who sins breaks the law; in fact, sin is lawlessness. [5] But you know that he appeared so that he might take away our sins. And in him is no sin.

Sin cannot be present where there is no law, and law is not necessary for a new creation that is already created to be the righteousness of God.

In Romans 8:1-2, Paul follows up this critical teaching: "There is, therefore, now no condemnation for those who are in Christ Jesus, because through Christ Jesus, the law of the Spirit of life has set us free from the law of sin and death."

These four truths are directly tied together. As a new creation in Christ, we were created in the image of God and endowed with His own righteousness and holiness. The law of God is written on our spiritual hearts. It is part of the DNA of our new spiritual identity.

> *There is no condemnation for those who are in Christ Jesus. (Romans 8:1)*

Because this is true, there is no need for external law; and, because there is no law, there is no transgression or sin.

The following diagram illustrates the stunning reality of our new spiritual identity:

TRUTH OF OUR NEW IDENTITY IN CHRIST

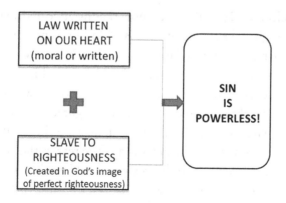

Even though we are no longer under law, we do not have a free license to let the sinful passions that remain present within our still fallen flesh find their place of dominance. God still desires for the fruit of our lives to be righteous. The difference, however, is that the fruit of that righteousness flows out of the transformation of God's work in our spirit, and it is, therefore, authentic and pleasing to God. Because we have been created as righteous and holy and are free from the control of law and sin, we are now enabled and fully empowered to allow the fruit of God's own righteousness to flow through us, rather than the self-generated filthy rags of our own righteousness that never had the ability to please God.

Following are a few more verses from 1 John as further affirmation of these points:

1 John 2:29 - If you know that he is righteous, you know that everyone who does what is right has been born of him.

1 John 3:5-10 - [5] But you know that he appeared so that he might take away our sins. And in him is no sin. [6] No one who lives in him keeps on sinning. No one who continues to sin has either seen him or known him. [7] Dear children, do not let anyone lead you astray. He who does what is right is righteous, *just as* he is righteous. [8] He who does what is sinful is of the devil, because the devil has been sinning from the beginning. The reason the Son of God appeared was to destroy the devil's work. [9] No one who is born of God will continue to sin, *because God's seed* *remains in him*; he cannot go on sinning, *because he has been born of God.* ¹⁰ This is how we know who the children of God are and who the children of the devil are: Anyone who does not do what is right is not a child of God; nor is anyone who does not love his brother.

1 John 3:24 - Those who obey his commands live in him, and he in them. And this is how we know that he lives in us: We know it by the Spirit he gave us.

1 John 5:1-5 - ¹ Everyone who believes that Jesus is the Christ is born of God, and everyone who loves the father loves his child as well. ² This is how we know that we love the children of God: by loving God and carrying out his commands. ³ This is love for God: to obey his commands. And his commands are not burdensome, ⁴ for everyone born of God overcomes the world. This is the victory that has overcome the world, even our faith. ⁵ Who is it that overcomes the world? Only he who believes that Jesus is the Son of God.

1 John 5:18-19 - ¹⁸ We know that anyone born of God does not continue to sin; the one who was born of God keeps him safe, and the evil one cannot harm him. ¹⁹ We know that we are children of God, and that the whole world is under the control of the evil one.

"To them (the Saints) God has chosen to make known
among the Gentiles the glorious riches of this mystery,
which is Christ in you, the hope of glory."
Colossians 1:26-27

CHAPTER 7

THE GREAT "RE"-UNION

What an amazing God we serve! He has done such a spectacular work inside of us; however, there is one more truth we must not overlook. When God created us as a brand new spirit and freed us from our personal enslavement to sin and death, He didn't then just step aside and leave it up to us to live out that new life on our own apart from Him. When He created us new again, He created us to once again share and enjoy intimate fellowship with Him, through His indwelling life and the infilling of His Spirit, united together with us in a magnificently vibrant relationship.

Created for Relationship

When God created man, He created us for a very special purpose. The Bible says we were created by God, for God, by His own will and for His own pleasure.

> **Revelation 4:11 (KJV)** - Thou art worthy, O Lord, to receive glory and honor and power: for thou hast created all things, and for thy pleasure they are and were created.[d]

That means that you and I were created, not only to reflect God's glory, but also for Him to enjoy. One of the many ways in which God enjoys His creation is through intimate relationship and fellowship. We see this exemplified in the Garden of Eden when God walked and talked with Adam and Eve in the cool of the day. He had created them as dependent creatures enabled by Him, and through Him, to enjoy friendship and community with Him and with one another. This vibrant relational experience has always been God's perfect blueprint for His creation. He made us in His image for that very reason.

The greatest deception recorded in Biblical history is the lie that we can have or keep God's glory apart from Him.

The Great Lie

The greatest deception recorded in Biblical history is the lie that we can have or keep God's glory apart from Him. The reason this lie is so devastating is that it completely contradicts the primary purpose for our existence which is to share in and enjoy a beautiful fulfilling relationship with our Creator.

Adam and Eve fell for this lie in the garden when the serpent said to them, "You will be *like God*, knowing good from evil." (Genesis 3:5) God had already created them in His perfect image with astounding splendor and glory. However, they were not created to be equal with God; rather, they were created as dependent beings for His own enjoyment and pleasure. He had created them to enjoy a rich and fulfilling relationship with Him. He set them in the garden and gave them work to do; but, though they were made in His image to reflect His glory, they were never intended to work alone, nor were they ever designed to experience or reflect God's glory apart from dependent union with Him. Because of their choice to believe the great lie of independence, the relationship which they enjoyed with their Creator was cataclysmically broken.

This great lie is what we also believed before our salvation, and it is the same lie to which our flesh often falls prey every time we believe that we can be like God, or even godly, apart from Him. The idea of dependence is something that is completely contrary to our fallen nature before Christ. As a matter of fact, the word "dependence" likely still invokes a negative fleshly response or cringe even among the saints. We must understand that we cannot maintain our own independence and experience the vibrant relationship God has intended us to share with Him, and with one another, at the same time. To do so, contradicts the very nature of God Himself and the primary purpose for which we were created.

Dependence, however, is not a bad word, especially when you see it in context of our beautiful relational God. Our dependence, in fact, is designed by God to draw us back again and again into the amazing relationship we were originally created to experience with Him.

The Ministry of Reconciliation

Let's look once more at 2 Corinthians 5:17-21:

> **2 Corinthians 5:17-21** - [17] Therefore, if anyone is in Christ, he is a new creation; the old has gone, the new has come! [18] All this is from God, who *reconciled* us to himself through Christ and gave us the ministry of *reconciliation*: [19] that God was reconciling the world to himself in Christ, not counting men's sins against them. And he has committed to us the message of reconciliation. [20] We are therefore Christ's ambassadors, as though God were making his appeal through us. We implore you on Christ's behalf: Be reconciled to God. [21] God made him who had no sin to be sin for us, so that in him we might become the righteousness of God.

Romans 5:10-11 says, "If, when we were God's enemies, we were reconciled to him through the death of his Son, how much more, having been reconciled, shall we be saved through his life!" Though the Greek word for "reconcile" literally means "to change" or "exchange,"[a] figuratively it means "the reestablishing of personal relations" or "to change from enmity to friendship."[e] The redeeming work of Christ had another astonishing consequence. Not only are we forgiven and set free from our enslavement to sin and not only have we been given eternal life, we have been restored to thoroughly enjoy an amazing personal relationship with our Creator. Why would the restoration of our relationship with God be so important to Him?

A Relational God

Consider the Trinity for a moment. God is One, but expresses Himself relationally in three distinct persons: Father, Son and Spirit. The personality of God represented through this triune relationship is truly extraordinary and demonstrates that at the heart of God is a passion for intimacy and community. Jesus declared that He and the Father are One. Throughout scripture, He testifies again and again to the beautiful unity shared between the Father, Son, and Spirit: one God in three persons. The Father is in the Son, and the Son is in the Father. The Son is in the Spirit, and the Spirit is in the Son. The Spirit is in the Father, and the

Father is in the Spirit. Scripture demonstrates that God exists communally with Himself in absolute perfect unity and divine order (John 5:19-23; 30; 8:25-30; 12:49-50; 14:9-11).

It is hard for us to imagine the fathomless depths of this relational God; yet, the astounding truth is that God has invited you and me to join in and partake of this holy relationship. Through His work of reconciliation through redemption, Jesus freed us from the effects of our own independence, and invited us back into a glorious *dependent* relationship with our Holy God.

> *God has invited us to join in and partake of this holy relationship.*

Now, as born-again new creations in Christ, we have once again been uniquely designed by Him for His own pleasure and enjoyment. How do we experience this supernatural dependent relationship with God today?

UNION WITH THE SPIRIT – I am in the Spirit and the Spirit is in Me

When Jesus left the earth in human form, he left us with an amazing gift. To understand the relational significance of this gift, we must first consider how man had experienced God prior to us receiving it. From the time of the Fall to the time of Christ, God's holy presence had only been experienced by His people from a great distance through terrifying encounters that made them tremble with fear. They watched those who approached God's presence without invitation or without proper cleansing be instantly struck down in death. God's intensely holy presence exposed and magnified their weakness and frailty, their sin and humanity in stark contradiction to His holy divine nature. You can likely imagine that they would not have perceived God to be one who desired intimacy and relationship with them.

Then a miracle happens as God moves a step closer to reconciliation with His creation. A baby is born named "Emmanuel" which means "God with us." He grew up and lived among us. He ate with us, drank with us, laughed and cried with us. He came in the humble form of a suffering servant, took on our own human likeness, and He allowed us to touch and see Him. In so doing, He revealed the relational love of the Father to us in ways that we would have never been able to see without Him. Jesus told us that to see Him is to see the Father.

Then, in His final words, He says:

John 14:16-17 - "[16] And I will ask the Father, and he will give you another Counselor to be with you forever — [17] the Spirit of truth. The world cannot accept him, because it neither sees him nor knows him. But you know him, for he lives with you and will be *in you*."

John 15:26 - "When the Counselor comes, whom I will send to you from the Father, the Spirit of truth who goes out from the Father, he will testify about me."

John 16:5-7 - "⁵ Now I am going to him who sent me, yet none of you asks me, 'Where are you going?' ⁶ Because I have said these things, you are filled with grief. ⁷ But I tell you the truth: It is for your good that I am going away. Unless I go away, the Counselor will not come to you; but if I go, I will send him to you.

Jesus understood that the relationship with the Counselor was necessary for us and that it would be the most wonderful relational experience with God that we could ever imagine; even better for us than Jesus' own physical presence in our world. No longer was God distant and untouchable due to sin and separation; instead, He was actively living inside of us, nurturing us, molding us and shaping us into His own likeness.

It is important to realize that this gift of the indwelling life of the Spirit inside of us comes from the Father at the request of the Son. God had planned this long ago. Remember, the prophet Ezekiel spoke of a time when we, as God's people, would receive a new heart and a new spirit through spiritual circumcision. This happened when we became a new creation in Christ. However, he also told us that something even greater would happen. He told us that in addition to being made new, we would also be enabled to enjoy the life and fellowship of God's own Spirit residing within us.

Ezekiel 36:26-27 - ²⁶ I will give you a new heart and put a new spirit in you; I will remove from you your heart of stone and give you a heart of flesh. ²⁷ And I will put my Spirit in you and move you to follow my decrees and be careful to keep my laws.

The Holy Spirit, also called the Counselor and Spirit of Truth, opens our eyes, ears, and minds to spiritual truth, always pointing us to Christ as our source. He helps us to recognize and accept truth. Then like a skillful Artisan, He undertakes the beautiful work of transforming us into the likeness and image of our Creator with ever-increasing glory through rebirth and regeneration.

John 3:5-8 - ⁵ Jesus answered, "I tell you the truth, no one can enter the kingdom of God unless he is born of water and the Spirit. ⁶ Flesh gives birth to flesh, but *the Spirit gives birth to spirit.* ⁷ You should not be surprised at my saying, 'You must be born again.' ⁸ The wind blows wherever it pleases. You hear its sound, but you cannot tell where it comes from or where it is going. So it is with everyone born of the Spirit."

John 16:12-15 - ¹² "I have much more to say to you, more than you can now bear. ¹³ But when he, the Spirit of truth, comes, he will guide you into all truth. He will not speak on his own; he will speak only what he hears, and he will tell you what is yet to come. ¹⁴ He will bring glory to me by taking from what is mine and making it known to you. ¹⁵ All that belongs to the Father is mine. That is why I said the Spirit will take from what is mine and make it known to you.

2 Corinthians 3:17-18 - [17] Now the Lord is the Spirit, and where the Spirit of the Lord is, there is freedom. [18] And we, who with unveiled faces all reflect the Lord's glory, are being transformed into his likeness with ever-increasing glory, which comes from the Lord, who is the Spirit.

I've often wondered what it would be like to see the intricacies of the Holy Spirit's personal interaction with us as His creation as He fashions and shapes us into a unique reflection of Himself. His work is extremely intimate, personal, and altogether wonderful. Though, in this life, we may never be fully aware of the incredibly intimate work of the Holy Spirit inside of us, we can be comforted in the fact that the Holy Spirit of God is ever-present, interceding for us, teaching and instructing us, encouraging us, drawing us toward Christ over and over again, and, ultimately, bringing us closer and closer to the fullness of God's glorious plans for our now and for our eternal future.

In reading this book so far, you may have noticed places where the Holy Spirit and our new spirit seem to have a great deal in common. This should not surprise us. After all, our new spirit was born of the Spirit of God. It was created by the Spirit in the image of God. Not only that, but our new spirit communes directly and regularly with the Holy Spirit, and the Holy Spirit has the amazing interpersonal work of bringing our spirit to full maturity by transforming us to eternal glory from the inside out.

2 Corinthians 4:16-17 - [16] Therefore we do not lose heart. Though outwardly we are wasting away, yet inwardly we are being renewed day by day. [17] For our light and momentary troubles are achieving for us an eternal glory that far outweighs them all.

Colossians 3:9-10 - [9] Do not lie to each other, since you have taken off your old self with its practices [10] and have put on the new self, which is being renewed in knowledge in the image of its Creator.

UNION WITH CHRIST – I am in Christ and Christ is in me.

In Colossians 1:26-27, Paul tells us that there was a great mystery that had been kept hidden for ages and generations, but this mystery has now been revealed to the saints. This mystery is the indwelling life of Christ in a believer: "Christ in you, the Hope of Glory."

Colossians 1:27 - "... to them *(the Saints)* God has chosen to make known among the Gentiles the glorious riches of this mystery, which is Christ in you, the hope of glory."

This is another precious and wonderfully profound truth found in scripture. No longer is Jesus Emmanuel, "God with us," now He is Christ in us. The glorious riches of this mystery again reveal to us a marvelously loving God who has gone through incredible lengths to reestablish His relationship with us.

Let's look at some of the last words of Jesus before His final arrest and crucifixion:

> **John 14:18-20** - [18] I will not leave you as orphans; I will come to you. [19] Before long, the world will not see me anymore, but you will see me. Because I live, you also will live. [20] On that day you will realize that *I am in my Father, and you are in me, and I am in you.*

> **John 17:24-26** - [24] "Father, I want those you have given me to be with me where I am, and to see my glory, the glory you have given me because you loved me before the creation of the world. [25] "Righteous Father, though the world does not know you, I know you, and they know that you have sent me. [26] I have made you known to them, and will continue to make you known in order that the *love you have for me may be in them and that I myself may be in them.*"

From the beginning of time, God has designed us for one amazing purpose: that is that we would enter *by choice* into a dynamically active and thriving dependent relationship with Him. The message of Christ in us is so powerful

> *God has designed us for one amazing purpose: that we would enter **by choice** into a dynamically active and thriving dependent relationship with Him.*

because it demonstrates a relational God that allows us, as His creation, to participate in His divine activity. He is in us, and we are in Him. As we become born-again, we are transformed out of our life of independence and separation into a life of beautiful dependence, where we are enabled to join in and participate in a beautiful intimate union with our Creator. Through this thriving dependent relationship, our Father empowers us to join with Him in full participation of all He is and does as He accomplishes His work and purposes in the earth. Therefore, every good and perfect spiritual work that He has for us to do can only be accomplished as we dependently live in Him and He lives in us.

> **Galatians 2:20** - I have been crucified with Christ and I no longer live, but Christ lives in me. The life I live in the body, I live by faith in the Son of God, who loved me and gave himself for me.

In John 15, Jesus paints a beautiful word picture of a branch to vine relationship to illustrate this active dependent relationship:

> **John 15:1-8** – "[1] I am the true vine, and my Father is the gardener. [2] He cuts off every branch in me that bears no fruit, while every branch that does bear fruit he prunes so that it will be even more fruitful. [3] You are already clean because of the word I have spoken to you. [4] Remain in me, and I will remain in you. No branch can bear fruit by itself; it must remain in the vine. Neither can you bear fruit unless you remain in me. [5] "I am the vine; you are the branches. If a man remains in me and I in him, he will bear much fruit; apart from me you can do nothing. [6] If anyone does not remain in me, he is like a branch that is thrown away and withers; such branches are picked up, thrown into the fire and burned. [7] If you remain in me

and my words remain in you, ask whatever you wish, and it will be given you. [8] This is to my Father's glory, that you bear much fruit, showing yourselves to be my disciples."

Because our fallen human flesh still retains that tendency toward independence and self-effort, when walking in the flesh, we often find ourselves still striving to attain success in our spiritual journey outside of Christ. We find it hard to rest and let go of our struggle and determination to do it on our own, or in our own way. The Word of God says that it is impossible for us to bear genuine fruit on our own apart from Christ. Therefore, when we are not actively living in the vine, we dry up and wither, our works are ineffective, and we find ourselves exhausted and worn out. Have you ever felt this way in your own walk with Christ? Most of us have at some point. Sometimes, we get so busy in our spiritual activity, taking on works that God never intended us to do, or at least that He didn't intend for us to do apart from Him. In those times, it is common to find ourselves walking through the independent self-effort of fallen flesh, rather than resting in the branch to vine relationship we have in Christ, allowing His life to flow in and through us. Walking in fleshly independence frequently leaves us feeling dry, parched, and barren in our spiritual activity, and it causes us to miss out on the rich abundant life we were always meant to share with Christ.

We need to realize that we cannot walk independent of God in our flesh and experience abundant life in the spirit at the same time. When we became a new spirit, our Father wired us in such a way that we will only truly experience His abundant life and spiritual victory as we learn to rest and abide in Him. He knew that if we were allowed to be successful through our own fleshly generated self-effort, we would completely bypass the vibrant relationship He has purposefully designed for us to share with Him. The abundant life experienced through this dependent relationship is better by far than any life we could ever experience through our own independence. Therefore, because of His great love, He saved us from the path of our own independence and has opened a new way of life unto us – life in the spirit, indwelled by the Holy Spirit and Christ. As we learn to walk in the spirit and embrace the dependent relationship we have with the Spirit and Christ, we find nourishment, fulfillment, and the most vibrant life we could ever imagine.

UNION WITH ONE ANOTHER – I am in You and You are in Me

So far, we have discovered the amazing unity that God shares within Himself communally as Father, Son, and Spirit. Then, we looked at how we each have been invited to participate in that divine unity as we are indwelled by the Holy Spirit and Christ.

Now, let's take this a step further. In God's perfect blueprint for His children, He also designed us to share in that *same union* with one another as brothers and sisters in Christ.

Let's take a closer look at the tender prayer of Jesus spoken to His Father only moments before He crossed the Kidron Valley to the Garden of Gethsemane. This amazing prayer, recorded in John 17:6-26, not only reveals the desire of God for His own relationship with us, but also reveals His plan and design for our relationship with one another.

> **John 17:6-11; 20-26** - [6] "I have revealed you to those whom you gave me out of the world. They were yours; you gave them to me and they have obeyed your word. [7] Now they know that everything you have given me comes from you. [8] For I gave them the words you gave me and they accepted them. They knew with certainty that I came from you, and they believed that you sent me. [9] I pray for them. I am not praying for the world, but for those you have given me, for they are yours. [10] All I have is yours, and all you have is mine. And glory has come to me through them. [11] I will remain in the world no longer, but they are still in the world, and I am coming to you. Holy Father, protect them by the power of your name—the name you gave me—*so that they may be one as we are one.* ... [20] "My prayer is not for them alone. I pray also for those who will believe in me through their message, [21] *that all of them may be one*, Father, *just as you are in me and I am in you.* May they also be in us *so that the world may believe* that you have sent me. [22] I have *given them the glory that you gave me, that they may be one as we are one:* [23] I in them and you in me. May they be brought to *complete*

unity to let the world know that you sent me and have loved them even as you have loved me. [24] "Father, I want those you have given me to be with me where I am, and to see my glory, the glory you have given me because you loved me before the creation of the world. [25] "Righteous Father, though the world does not know you, I know you, and they know that you have sent me. [26] I have made you known to them, and will continue to make you known in order that the *love you have for me may be in them* and that *I myself may be in them*."

Notice the words "just as" and "as" found in verses 11, 21, and 22. The unity God has intended for us, as His children, is not just any kind of superficial oneness. Jesus' prayer to the Father is that you and I be one in the *same way* that He, the Father, and the Spirit are one. How can that be? I don't know about you, but I see very little of this among God's people these days. We still have very individual and independent agendas, not only across denominational lines, but even within our own local church body. Far too often, our disunity has had the profoundly opposite effect of driving the world away from the message of Christ, rather than pointing them to the truth that He was sent by the Father. Disunity in the body of Christ brings the validity of Christ's message into question. Please understand that it is not my intention to lay a foundation for guilt here; however, I do believe that God will answer Jesus' prayer. I do believe that there is something more to come to the body of Christ when it comes to experiencing unity with one another, and I believe it is something that we must be "brought to" by the hand of God.

Perhaps, one reason we haven't experienced the full measure of this unity within the body is because we have not understood and believed the spiritual truths about regeneration even within ourselves, much less within one another. We still look at one another through the eyes of our fallen flesh. In so doing, we only see fallen flesh looking back at us. In 2 Corinthians 5:16, Paul writes "So from now on, we regard no one from a worldly point of view." This statement is in context with his explanation of what it means to be a new spirit living inside of an earthly tent. As we begin to recognize and accept the realities of our own personal spiritual transformation in Christ, we are better enabled to recognize that same transformation is occurring in other believers as well. The bottom line is that we all have issues with our flesh tent, and sometimes our own flesh, or the flesh of other brothers and sisters around us, shouts so loud it prevents us from seeing one another as righteous new-born creations of our Holy God, fully loved, and fully accepted by Him. However, as we begin to experience more and more what it is like to walk in the glorious unity we have with the Father, Son, and Spirit, and as we begin to see ourselves truly as God created us and learn to walk in that truth, I believe it will have the profound impact of transforming our view of one another as well.

In God's design for His creation, He made us dependent on Him and upon each other. Though each one of us is individually created in His image with specific design and purpose, we are not created to do anything alone. We need God. We need each other. Because of this, the Holy Spirit has uniquely equipped each of us for our part in God's work. Not only that, but He comes alongside of us in power and authority. He lives in us and lives through us, expressing Himself uniquely through every individual in the body of Christ. We were never designed to do it alone. Jesus is the head, and we are His body, members fitly joined together under the headship of Christ. As individual parts of the body, we all function together to accomplish His plans and purposes on this Earth.

We were never designed to do it alone.

Right now, take a moment to meditate on how much you are loved by the Father. Consider the amazing lengths your God has gone through to re-establish His relationship with you. You are thoroughly loved. Is there anyone in your life that you are currently seeing from a "worldly point of view?" If so, I encourage you to pray through this, and ask God to reveal them to you through spiritual eyes.

I pray that we all will find the deepest place of communion and trust in this intimate dynamic relationship with our Holy God and with one another.

*"For we are God's workmanship, created in Christ Jesus
to do good works, which God prepared in advance for us to do."*
Ephesians 2:10

CHAPTER 8

THE SKILLFUL ARTISAN

Hopefully, by now you are realizing that God has created you as something very special. Isaiah 64:8 declares that we are the work of God's hand.

Isaiah 64:8 – Yet, O Lord, you are our Father. We are the clay, you are the potter; we are all the work of your hand.

Your Father has created you to partake in His own divine nature, His own righteousness, and His own holiness. You are His sweet creation, a favored child, and dearly loved. As such, He has imparted to you many of His own divine qualities. He has created you and equipped you uniquely for His own purposes. He has not left you alone to carry them out; instead, He has joined in a beautiful union and fellowship with you to accomplish His work in and through you.

Spiritual Plans & Callings

The Bible says that our new spirit has work to do and that God has prepared these works in advance for us to accomplish.

> **Ephesians 2:10** - For we are God's workmanship, created in Christ Jesus to do good works, which God prepared in advance for us to do.

While in this fallen body and on this fallen earth, we face a struggle. There is a world around us that does not know God. In his letter to the Philippians, Paul wrote that, although he desired to depart and be with Christ, he knew it was essential for him to remain in the body a little longer for the progress and joy of others in the faith (Philippians 1:20-26). We can be confident that if we are a believer in Christ, breathing air on this earth, God is not done with us just yet. The fact that we have life is proof that God has a purpose for us to remain for a season in this fallen body so that we may carry out all the works He has ordained for us to do. The beautiful truth is that God already knows what those works are, and the Holy Spirit is presently intimately at work within our own spirit to help us discern those works and perform them to God's own glory. We must recognize, however, that it is not up to us to figure out what that work is and attempt to accomplish it on our own apart from God. Rather, as we learn to walk as a new creation in Christ and in the fullness of what He has done inside of us, and as we let go of human effort and striving, we will find ourselves right in the middle of His plans, fully empowered and enabled to accomplish them.

Since early childhood, I had always felt there was a calling and purpose for my life. I haven't always known exactly what that calling or purpose was, but I knew what I felt had been put there by God. Often, I lived in great anxiety and fear that I would miss His plans for me and disappoint Him in some way. Then, as God slowly began to reveal His plans to me, I struggled with even greater fear. My fear was based in what I could best quantify as "my own abilities." I felt weak, insignificant, small in light of the accomplishments of others I saw around me, and I often focused more on all the human reasons why I could not possibly be used to accomplish what He had called me to do. I am a woman. I didn't finish college or go to seminary. I was overweight, short, etc. The list goes on. But I knew deep within my spirit that God had a purpose for my life, and I knew, with certainty, I didn't want to miss out on it. Over time, I realized that many of my beliefs and thoughts were not of God. I was focusing on fleshly realities, rather than spiritual. Slowly, I began to realize that if God had called me for His purposes, He would have to be the One to accomplish them through me. I realized that apart from Him, I had very little to offer. So, as the story of the boy with the five loaves and two fish, I offered the little bit I thought I had and asked Him to take it and do whatever it was He wanted to do. Then came the hard part ... I had to let go. I will tell you that there have been many times when I attempted to reach out to give that offering to Him only to retract my hands out of fear that what I was giving wasn't enough. Over time, He began to open my heart and mind to understand the spiritual truths I have shared with you, and He helped me to realize that He has already given me everything I need to accomplish His work. However, that which He gave me came from a different place than the flesh I was living in. It came through the righteous new spirit that He had made me to be, indwelled and empowered by the living resurrected Son of God and the dynamic Holy Spirit. If this is true for me, it is true for all of God's children. Whatever calling or purpose God has put within your spirit, you must know that He has already uniquely and perfectly equipped you to accomplish it through Him.

Spiritual Gifts and Talents

When we became new-born creations of Christ, created in His image, God did not make us as cookie-cutter versions of Himself. Each of us was individually skillfully crafted at the hands of the

Master Artisan with a unique purpose and style of reflecting His glory. We are each created with different functions and purpose, with unique personalities, gifts, and talents. Scripture says that He has given each one of us different gifts or manifestations of the Spirit according to His grace.

> **Romans 12:4-8** - [4] Just as each of us has one body with many members, and these members do not all have the same function, [5] so in Christ we who are many form one body, and *each member belongs to all the others.* [6] We have different gifts, *according to the grace given us.* If a man's gift is prophesying, let him use it in proportion to his faith. [7] If it is serving, let him serve; if it is teaching, let him teach; [8] if it is encouraging, let him encourage; if it is contributing to the needs of others, let him give generously; if it is leadership, let him govern diligently; if it is showing mercy, let him do it cheerfully.

> **1 Corinthians 12:4-13** - [4] There are different kinds of gifts, but the same Spirit. [5] There are different kinds of service, but the same Lord. [6] There are different kinds of working, but the same God works all of them in all men. [7] Now to each one the manifestation of the Spirit is given *for the common good.* [8] To one there is given through the Spirit the message of wisdom, to another the message of knowledge by means of the same Spirit, [9] to another faith by the same Spirit, to another gifts of healing by that one Spirit, [10] to another miraculous powers, to another prophecy, to another distinguishing between spirits, to another speaking in different kinds of tongues, and to still another the interpretation of tongues. [11] All these are the work of one and the same Spirit, and he gives them to each one, *just as he determines.* [12] The body is a unit,

though it is made up of many parts; and though all its parts are many, they form one body. So it is with Christ. [13] For we were all baptized by one Spirit into one body— whether Jews or Greeks, slave or free—and we were all given the one Spirit to drink.

Gifts, talents, and abilities are given to each of us by the Spirit as He determines. Notice, however, that they are not given to us for our own good, but for the good of one another. In other words, the gifts the Spirit has given me belong to you; and, the gifts He has given you belong to me. Praise God! In that way, God created the whole body of Christ to share an amazing unity with one another through that same dependent relationship we share with Him. All of our gifts are intended for mutual edification, building up, and encouragement of others in the Lord.

Ephesians 4:11-16 - [11] It was he who gave some to be apostles, some to be prophets, some to be evangelists, and some to be pastors and teachers, [12] to prepare God's people for works of service, so that the body of Christ may be built up [13] until we all reach unity in the faith and in the knowledge of the Son of God and become mature, attaining to the whole measure of the fullness of Christ. [14] Then we will no longer be infants, tossed back and forth by the waves, and blown here and there by every wind of teaching and by the cunning and craftiness of men in their deceitful scheming. [15] Instead, speaking the truth in love, we will in all things grow up into him who is the Head, that is, Christ. [16] From him the whole body, joined and held together by every supporting ligament, grows and builds itself up in love, as each part does its work.

Throughout scripture, there is a direct correlation between the gifts of the spirit and the unity of the body of Christ. We are created to enjoy fellowship with one another. We are created in such a way that we need one another. Each of us has a part that contributes to the whole of God's work. Only together, in Christ, do we become a beautiful tapestry of design reflecting our Lord and Savior to the world around us.

> *Only together, in Christ, do we become a beautiful tapestry of design reflecting our Lord and Savior to the world around us.*

Notice the goal of the gifts given to apostles, prophets, evangelists, pastors, and teachers is to prepare God's people for works of service, *so that* the body of Christ may be built up. Verse 13 tells us that the plan of God through these gifts will be unity in the faith and in the knowledge of Christ, and spiritual maturity for the body, so that we both individually, and as Christ's body, may attain to the *whole measure* of Christ's fullness. What an astounding result!

Spiritual Power

Gifts and talents are wonderful, as is our spiritual calling; yet, without the power of God behind them, they remain ineffective.

In Acts 1:8, Jesus told His disciples that they would receive power when the Holy Spirit came on them. The spiritual power that God gave them is also for us today as a new creation in Christ. The Word of God says that we have been given a spirit of power, love, and self-discipline.

> **2 Timothy 1:6-7 -** [6] For this reason I remind you to fan into flame the gift of God, which is in you through the laying on of my hands. [7] For God did not give us a spirit of timidity, but a spirit of *power*, of love and of self-discipline.

The Greek word for power is *dunamis*. It means "inherent power, or power residing in a thing by virtue of its nature."[a] Harper's Bible Dictionary defines the word power as "the actual or potential capacity to effect something by virtue of inherent excellence or rightful authority."[f] As a new creation in Christ, we have both the power and the rightful authority to effect the world around us because of the inherent qualities of God's own power residing within us, as we abide in Him and He in us. This means we have all the power we need to fight the good fight of faith and to accomplish all that God has for us to do on this earth. Ephesians 6:10 instructs us to "be strong in the Lord and in His mighty power," and to take our stand not against flesh and blood, but against the rulers, authorities, and powers of this dark world, and against the spiritual forces of evil in the heavenly realms. Satan knows that our new spirit is incredibly powerful and dangerous to the Kingdom of Darkness, and he does not want us to grasp the truth of it. Applied knowledge and understanding of these truths about our newly created spirit are powerful tools in our ultimate war against the powers and principalities of darkness in this world.

Perhaps like me, you have felt called by God to do something you perceive to be "beyond yourself." I want to encourage you today to realize that if Christ is in you, and the Holy Spirit is in you as a newly created spirit in Christ, you do not lack anything! You have all the power you need, all the resources you need, all the abilities you need, all the talent you need, and anything else you need to be perfect in your walk with Christ, and to perfectly fulfill all that He desires for you to do. These things, however, cannot be synthetically generated out of our fallen flesh that lives independent of God. Rather, they are only experienced as we live life in the spirit, united with the Spirit and Christ, in beautiful union and relational fellowship with God and with each other.

> **2 Peter 1:3-4 -** [3] His divine power has given us everything we need for life and godliness through our knowledge of him who called us by his own glory and goodness. [4] Through these he has given us his very great and precious promises, so that through them you may participate in the divine nature and escape the corruption in the world caused by evil desires.

*"We have not received the spirit of the world
but the Spirit who is from God, that we may
understand what God has freely given us."*
1 Corinthians 2:12

CHAPTER 9

"MIND, WILL, & EMOTIONS
... OH MY"

Throughout history, many theories among philosophers,
theologians, and scientists have arisen attempting to
describe the interaction between the human body and spirit.
Our human reasoning is limited, especially when it comes to
describing those things that are unseen or eternal. So, what does
scripture tell us about where the invisible qualities of our mind,
will, and emotions dwell? Is it in the body, or in the spirit, or do
these qualities live in some completely separate part of us?

After seeking the word on this topic, I believe that there is
both scriptural and scientific evidence to support that our body, or

flesh tent, has its own mind, will, and emotions; yet, we, as spirit, have a spiritual mind, will and emotions as well.

The Carnal Mind vs. The Spiritual Mind

The carnal mind is where human logic and reasoning occur. Everything we take into it is filtered through the sum of our past experiences, our memories both good and bad, the habits and patterns that we have developed through the years even when we were still walking in our old sin nature before Christ. Our thoughts are influenced by our education, our exposure to various teaching, our upbringing, and our peers. All in all, our carnal mind is a jumbled up mix of both positive and negative exposure that builds up throughout our lifetime. All new information that it takes in is filtered through this mix.

Our carnal mind is unspiritual and of broken, earthly, perishable material. Because of this, it is resistant to understanding and assimilating the things of the spirit. Therefore, we are taught in scripture to renew the mind again and again of spiritual realities regarding our true identity in Christ. Day by day, and even moment by moment, we must choose to "put on" all that God has made us to be. Without this continuous renewal, our brain quickly defaults back to its old flesh patterns, thoughts, and habits. When we let it go unchecked for a while, without going through the intentional process of renewing it in the truth, our carnal mind begins to seek ways to usurp authority and dominance until we make the deliberate choice to bring it back under submission to all that God has made us to be on the inside.

Scripture says that we, however, as spirit have been given a different mind ... the mind of Christ.

1 Corinthians 2:6-16 - [6] We do, however, speak a message of wisdom among the mature, but not the wisdom of this age or of the rulers of this age, who are coming to nothing. [7] No, we speak of God's secret wisdom, a wisdom that has been hidden and that God destined for our glory before time began. [8] None of the rulers of this age understood it, for if they had, they would not have crucified the Lord of glory. [9] However, as it is written: "No eye has seen, no ear has heard, no mind has conceived what God has prepared for those who love him" [10] but God has revealed it to us by his Spirit. The Spirit searches all things, even the deep things of God. [11] For who among men knows the thoughts of a man except the man's spirit within him? In the same way no one knows the thoughts of God except the Spirit of God. [12] We have not received the spirit of the world but the Spirit who is from God, that we may understand what God has freely given us. [13] This is what we speak, not in words taught us by human wisdom but in words taught by the Spirit, expressing spiritual truths in spiritual words. [14] The man without the Spirit does not accept the things that come from the Spirit of God, for they are foolishness to him, and he cannot understand them, because they are spiritually discerned. [15] The spiritual man makes judgments about all things, but he himself is not subject to any man's judgment: [16] "For who has known the mind of the Lord that he may instruct him?" But we have the mind of Christ.

As spirit, we have been given the spiritual mind of Christ so that we may understand what God has freely given us, those things that he has planned for *our glory* since before time began. Notice that these things are not understood through the natural or carnal mind, but through the spiritual mind of Christ as our spiritual mind communes directly with the mind of the Holy Spirit, and as the Holy Spirit communes directly with the mind of the Father. When we seek to discern truth through the lens of our carnal mind, we most often miss the mark because the truth we are taking in is being filtered through the jumbled up blend of our past experience, habits, and carnal thought patterns.

> *As spirit, we have been given the spiritual mind of Christ*

Verse 15 tells us that another reason we have been given the spiritual mind of Christ is so that we can make spiritual judgments. We live in a day and age where making judgments is not considered politically correct; nonetheless, this verse says that our new spirit has been given the mind of Christ so that it can make spiritual judgments. The Greek word used here for "judge" is *anakrino* which means "to seek to learn the truth by careful study, to evaluate carefully, to examine or judge."[a] Now let me be sure to clarify that we are talking about the mind of Christ given to the newly created spirit for the purpose of making spiritual judgments. Judgments made through the mind of fallen flesh are entirely different than judgments that flow from the spiritual mind of Christ. One way to measure the source of our judgment is to look at how Christ walked while on this earth. If our judgments look different than His, it is unlikely we are using the spiritual mind of Christ to make them.

As a side note here, this passage also declares that we are not subject to any man's judgment. Why would this be true? It is true because, as we have learned, our spirit has been created by God to be like God in true righteousness and holiness. Therefore, our new spirit has already been "credited" with righteousness, or deemed and judged as righteous by God. Colossians 1:21-23 tells us that in God's sight, we are holy and without blemish, free from accusation.

> **Colossians 1:21-23** - [21] Once you were alienated from God and were enemies in your minds because of your evil behavior. [22] But now he has reconciled you by Christ's physical body through death to present you holy in his sight, without blemish and free from accusation— [23] if you continue in your faith, established and firm, not moved from the hope held out in the gospel. This is the gospel that you heard and that has been proclaimed to every creature under heaven, and of which I, Paul, have become a servant.

If God has created us as a brand new righteous and holy representation of Himself, and His judgment of us is that we are righteous, then what can any man say against the declaration of God. There is no higher authority than God's judgment. This should provide a great source of rest for us as we experience the insults and attacks of others. We are fully accepted, loved, and approved by the Almighty God of the universe. No other judgment against us matters.

The mind of our spirit has been created to readily accept and assimilate spiritual truth; yet, it is the unwieldy, cumbersome, carnal mind of our flesh that often presents us with its deceptive arguments. As long as we live in the tent of this body of broken flesh, we must be persistent in teaching and training our carnal minds to accept spiritual realities regarding our true spiritual identity.

The Carnal Will vs. The Spiritual Will

We already covered in Chapter 5 that our flesh has its own will and appetite that operates in direct opposition to the will of God found in our spirit. As a reminder, our new spirit has been created to delight in God's law (Romans 7:14-25). Scripture says that as spirit, we have the law of God written on our hearts and minds (Jeremiah 31:33; Hebrews 10:15-16). This means that we have already been created to be in complete agreement with the will of

God, to walk in righteousness and holiness in full obedience to all of God's laws. The "want to" or "desire" toward righteousness is already part of the DNA of our new spirit. There is no contradiction between the will of our new spirit and the righteous requirements of God's law because our new spirit has been awarded God's own righteousness, and is, therefore, already in perfect agreement with God's will. Conversely, however, Romans 8:5-8 tells us that the carnal mind, or mind of the flesh, remains hostile toward God; therefore, it is not able to submit to God's law.

Romans 8:5-8 – [5] Those who live according to the sinful nature (or flesh) have their minds set on what that nature desires; but those who live in accordance with the Spirit have their minds set on what the Spirit desires. [6] The mind of sinful man (or mind of the flesh) is death, but the mind controlled by the Spirit is life and peace; [7] the sinful mind (or mind set on the flesh) is hostile to God. It does not submit to God's law, nor can it do so. [8] Those controlled by the sinful nature (or flesh) cannot please God.

This passage says that as spirit, we already desire what the Spirit desires. It is our flesh tent that, when given the opportunity, asserts itself toward its own independent will in direct opposition to God's perfect law. We must remember that, as a new creation in Christ, we are no longer controlled or dominated by the will of the flesh which produces death, but by the will of the Spirit which produces life and peace.

Carnal Emotions vs. Spiritual Emotions

This is a sticky one to unravel because so much of what we typically consider to be our identity ties directly to our emotional responses. We have already learned that the physical brain, or carnal mind, houses many aspects of human emotion, and that physical trauma, as well as hormonal and chemical changes within our brain, can magnify our awareness of this fact. Trauma to certain areas of the brain can cause a person to be emotionally catatonic. Feelings of depression, anxiety, and hopelessness are often linked to specific chemical or hormonal imbalances in the brain. Depending on the root cause, certain medications or nutritional aids can often be introduced into the body to help curb and relieve the symptoms of severe emotional swings. With this understanding, we can determine that at least part of our human emotional response is tied directly to the physical brain which we already know is part of our fallen flesh. Again, we must be reminded that our body is broken. It is not what God originally planned for us from the beginning. Because of this, fleshly emotions often blind us from the truth.

Fleshly emotions include such things as hatred, fear, anxiety, worry, insecurity, bitterness, jealousy, malice and rage. These emotional responses are not part of our new nature in Christ, but remnants carried over from our old sin nature that remain present within the fallen flesh tent in which we live. These fleshly emotional responses can be powerfully deceptive, and often prevent our carnal minds from accepting the truth of our new identity in Christ.

In Galatians 5:17-26, Paul contrasts the differences between emotions belonging to the flesh and those belonging to us as spirit.

> **Galatians 5:17-26** - [17] For the sinful nature (flesh) desires what is contrary to the Spirit, and the Spirit what is contrary to the sinful nature (flesh). They are in conflict with each other, so that you do not do what you want. [18] But if you are led by the Spirit, you are not under law. [19] The acts of the sinful nature (flesh) are obvious: sexual immorality, impurity and debauchery; [20] idolatry and witchcraft; hatred, discord, jealousy, fits of rage, selfish ambition, dissensions, factions [21] and envy; drunkenness, orgies, and the like. I warn you, as I did before, that those who live like this will not inherit the kingdom of God. [22] But the fruit of the Spirit is love, joy, peace, patience, kindness, goodness, faithfulness, [23] gentleness and self-control. Against such things there is no law. [24] Those who belong to Christ Jesus have crucified the sinful nature (flesh) with its passions and desires. [25] Since we live by the Spirit, let us keep in step with the Spirit. [26] Let us not become conceited, provoking and envying each other.

Notice that the acts of the flesh, as well as the fruit of the spirit, both include emotional components within their respective lists. For example, under the list of the emotional fruit of the spirit, we find love, joy, and peace. Conversely, the list of *"acts of the flesh,"* includes the human emotional responses of hatred, jealousy, rage, selfishness, and envy.

It is usually not too hard for us to identify when we are experiencing these negative emotions of the flesh. However, did you know that fleshly emotions do not always appear negative? In the independence of our flesh, we often attempt to mimic or imitate positive emotions as well. For example, have you ever tried to cultivate through your own efforts the emotions of love, joy, or peace? How did that work for you? Our fleshly attempts at producing these emotions may at times give us a feeling of some measure of independent success in our spiritual walk. The problem, however, is that man-made fruit never truly satisfies those who partake of it. Synthetic fruit never tastes as good as the real thing. Therefore, God never intended this emotional fruit to be manufactured through the self-effort of fallen flesh; rather, it is only genuinely produced as we walk in the spirit, indwelled by the Spirit and Christ.

> *Man-made fruit never truly satisfies those who partake of it.*

Let's take the emotional fruit of love as an example. Christ commands us to love others.

John 15:12 - My command is this: Love each other *as I have loved you.*

Take a moment and think about how you love your spouse, your family, your friends, your brothers and sisters in Christ, and even your enemies. Does your love measure up to the standard of loving them the *same as* Christ loved you? If you take this command out of context, loving as Christ loved us would seem like an impossible thing to do. So often, when we are living out of the independence of our flesh, we take Christ's command to love, and then add our own fleshly mix of self-effort and striving to it, trying as hard as we can to love in the way we think God wants us to love others. We find, however, that our fleshly attempts to synthetically produce the fruit of love fail miserably, and we never really measure up to the perfect standard of loving others in the *same way* Christ loved us. So, let's now look at this command to love within its proper scriptural context.

Christ's command to love as, or in the same way as, He loved us is found in context of the branch to vine relationship that we have already examined in John 15:1-8. As a reminder, Jesus tells us that He is the true vine, and that when we remain in Him, and He in us, through the beautiful dependent relationship He has made us to experience with Him, we will bear much fruit.

Then, starting in verse 9, Jesus uses His command to love as the perfect example of what it looks like to bear genuine fruit as we abide in the vine:

John 15:9-12 - [9] "*As* the Father has loved me, *so* have I loved you. Now remain in my love. [10] If you obey my commands, you will remain in my love, *just as* I have obeyed my Father's commands and remain in his love. [11] I have told you this so that my joy may be in you and that your joy may be complete. [12] My command is this: Love each other *as I have loved you*.

It is essential to grasp that this passage says that the love the Father has for the Son is the *exact same love* that the Son has for us. Jesus was the perfect model of abiding in the vine. He didn't *try* to emulate love *like* the Father through effort and striving; He actually loved with the *same love* of the Father. You might say, "Well sure. He was God, so it wouldn't be hard for Him to love with the same love as the Father." But look closely at what He is saying here. He said he obeyed His Father's commands and *remained in* His love. Because of that, He was able to allow the perfect love of the Father to flow to Him and through Him. Then, He tells us that when we abide in Him and *remain in* His love, we too are enabled to love others with that *exact same* love. So instead of this passage being an impossible standard of love to which we need to measure up, we find it is a source for perfect love in which we need to abide through the dependent relationship we have as spirit with our Creator.

The reality is that love synthetically produced through the independent will and mind of our broken flesh is contaminated;

and, therefore, it will never compare or measure up to the perfect and pure love of God. We must recognize that there is only one love, and it is God's great pleasure to share it both to and through His creation. It is only as we learn to walk as the new spirit that we are, already made perfect in love, that the fruit of perfect true love can be fully displayed through us. However, that love is not just any kind of love. It is the divine, perfect, holy love of God Himself, and because it is God's love, it has profound results in the lives of individuals who partake of it.

> **John 15:13-17 -** [13] Greater love has no one than this, that he lay down his life for his friends. [14] You are my friends if you do what I command. [15] I no longer call you servants, because a servant does not know his master's business. Instead, I have called you friends, for everything that I learned from my Father I have made known to you. [16] You did not choose me, but I chose you and appointed you to go and bear fruit—fruit that will last. Then the Father will give you whatever you ask in my name. [17] This is my command: Love each other.

> **1 John 4:7-12 -** [7] Dear friends, let us love one another, for love comes from God. Everyone who loves has been born of God and knows God. [8] Whoever does not love does not know God, because God is love. [9] This is how God showed his love among us: He sent his one and only Son into the world that we might live through him. [10] This is love: not that we loved God, but that he loved us and sent his Son as an atoning sacrifice for our sins. [11] Dear friends, since God so loved us, we also ought to love one another.

[12] No one has ever seen God; but if we love one another, God lives in us and his love is made complete in us.

1 Peter 1:22-23 - [22] Now that you have purified your-selves by obeying the truth so that you have sincere love for your brothers, love one another deeply, from the heart. [23] For you have been born again, not of perishable seed, but of imperishable, through the living and enduring word of God.

Notice how often the exhortation for us to love found in scripture is directly tied to our new spiritual identity and depen-dent relationship with God.

The example of love found in the branch to vine relationship is an amazing demonstration of how God's Spirit, present within our own spirit, can produce the pure and genuine emotional fruit of love. The same truth applies to all of the other emotional fruits of the spirit as well. The only way we can experience or exhibit genuine joy, peace, patience, kindness, goodness, faithfulness, gen-tleness, and self-control is when we are walking in the spirit, living relationally in the vine as a new born creation of God, allowing His own attributes of love, joy, peace, patience, kindness, good-ness, faithfulness, gentleness, and self-control to flow both to us and through us. Can you imagine if all who professed belief in Christ could simply walk in this one truth?

As we examine closely what the Bible teaches about the mind, will, and emotions of the flesh in contrast to the mind, will, and emotions of the spirit, we must again always bear in mind that we are no longer identified in our fallen flesh. We do not have two natures. Therefore, our only nature is found in the truth of who God has made us to be as a new spirit.

> **Romans 8:9-11 -** [9]You, however, are controlled not by the sinful nature [or flesh] but by the Spirit, if the Spirit of God lives in you. And if anyone does not have the Spirit of Christ, he does not belong to Christ. [10] But if Christ is in you, your body is dead because of sin, yet your spirit is alive because of righteousness. [11] And if the Spirit of him who raised Jesus from the dead is living in you, he who raised Christ from the dead will also give life to your mortal bodies through his Spirit, who lives in you.

For now, nonetheless, the fact is we still live in the tent of fallen flesh. For that reason, it is helpful to understand our fleshly responses, as well as spiritual, so that we can discern what we are walking in at a given moment. Therefore, as frustrating as our carnal mind, will, and emotions can be, let us retain three very important truths:

1. Our carnal mind, will, and emotions do not define our true identity.

2. Our carnal mind, will, and emotions can be renewed in the truth and brought under submission to who we really are in Christ.

3. Our carnal mind, will, and emotions are part of our temporary broken flesh and will not continue with us when we die.

"I have been crucified with Christ and I no longer live,
but Christ lives in me. The life I live in the body,
I live by faith in the Son of God, who loved me
and gave himself for me."
Galatians 2:20

CHAPTER 10

A CHOICE TO DIE

———❦———

Have you ever fallen into an area of sin only to find yourself hitting rock bottom? In that place of desperation, you cry out to God asking Him to get you out of your mess, bartering with grand promises to Him of how you will do better, try harder, and do more for Him. Then, in your flesh, you pick yourself up and you strive as hard as you can to follow through on your promises to God only to find you eventually can't keep up your end of the bargain. Exhausted, frustrated, and usually ridden with guilt, you fall harder and make even bigger promises and repeat this pattern over and over.

As believers, we often try to fight the deeds and cravings of our flesh with our flesh. In other words, we try to work out of the limited resources of the flesh to force the type of fleshly compliance we desire. This approach at correcting the behavior of the flesh never works as any long-term solution because there is no real power in it. We must realize that the flesh can never accomplish a purifying work within itself. In this life, the flesh remains fallen and corrupt. It will only be made perfect when we receive our new glorified bodies at the resurrection. This means that all of our efforts at fixing the flesh are futile. For some, this might be a shocking statement because we have all heard a lifetime of Sunday 4-point sermons that have directed us over and over on how to fix that which is eternally broken.

So the obvious question is posed, "Do we just let the sin in our flesh run its course?" Of course not, however, scripture does not teach us to fix that which is eternally broken; it teaches us to die to it. There is nothing wrong with teaching what the misdeeds of the flesh are. Much of scripture is given to this. However, if the sole focus of our teaching is directed at fixing the flesh from the outside in, rather than dying to it, we have missed one of the most

> *Scripture does not teach us to fix that which is eternally broken; it teaches us to die to it.*

critical precepts found in the gospel. So the real question we should be asking is, "How do we live inside of broken flesh and not allow the sin still present within it to dominate our lives?" Scripture plainly presents the answer to this fundamentally important question.

Live by the Spirit.

> **Galatians 5:16** - So, I say, live by the Spirit, and you will not gratify the desires of the sinful nature (flesh).

As a matter of basic and simple truth, Paul states that if we are living by the spirit, we will not gratify or give in to the cravings of our fallen flesh. Day by day, moment by moment, we must choose to walk in the truth of who we are as spirit, rather than the truth of our broken flesh. As we walk in the generous freedom that has been afforded to us as a new spirit, the sin in our flesh becomes dormant allowing us to truly live the rich abundant life God intended for us to live while we walk on this earth in this body.

As we live in the spirit, we must always be aware that the flesh is ever-present, looking for any opportunity to raise its ugly head and find a place of dominance in our lives; yet, scripture tells us that as we walk in the spirit, our flesh will be brought under the submission and direction of its new tenant. It will be dominated and rendered ineffective, and we will be fully enabled and empowered to put to death the misdeeds of our body.

Romans 8:12-13 - [12] Therefore, brothers, we have an obligation—but it is not to the sinful nature (flesh), to live according to it. [13] For if you live according to the sinful nature (flesh), you will die; but if by the Spirit you put to death the misdeeds of the body, you will live,

So the next question arises, "How does one live by the Spirit?" Again, the Bible provides some very clear and specific answers.

Take off the "old self" and put on the "new self."

Ephesians 4:22-24 - [22] You were taught, with regard to your former way of life, to put off your old self, which is being corrupted by its deceitful desires; [23] to be made new in the attitude of your minds; [24] and to put on the new self, created to be like God in true righteousness and holiness.

We have already looked at this verse several times, but how do we "put on" something that we already are? After all, we are new creations in Christ: the old has gone, the new has come. Therefore, why do we need to keep taking off the old and keep putting on the new? The key to answering this question is *"to be made new in the attitude of your minds."* The truth of being a new creation is an absolute reality, but so is the carnal mind of the flesh. We must choose to actively and deliberately teach and train our carnal minds to understand, believe, and accept the spiritual realities concerning our relationship to God and Christ.

Count yourselves as dead to sin and alive to God.

> **Romans 6:11-14** - [11] In the same way, count yourselves
> dead to sin but alive to God in Christ Jesus. [12] Therefore
> do not let sin reign in your mortal body so that you obey
> its evil desires. [13] Do not offer the parts of your body to
> sin, as instruments of wickedness, but rather offer your-
> selves to God, as those who have been brought from death
> to life; and offer the parts of your body to him as instru-
> ments of righteousness. [14] For sin shall not be your master,
> because you are not under law, but under grace.

Though we are aware that sin is still present in our fallen flesh, we should consider ourselves as dead to sin because this is the truth of who we are. Remember, that word "count" in the Greek means "to deem as, determine as, judge as having the like force and weight of something." Therefore, as we consider ourselves as having the like force and weight of being dead to sin, we keep sin in the flesh from usurping control. As we walk in the spirit, the members of our fallen body can then be offered to God as instruments of righteousness. For example, our mouth can be offered to declare His word and to bring encouragement and exhortation to others. Our hands can be used to serve others in love. Our eyes can be used to see the needs of others around us. We enable the members of our body, each and every part, to be used to effectively serve God's righteous purposes on the earth.

Conversely, when we don't count ourselves as dead to sin, we tend to live with the focus of trying to fix our broken flesh by imposing continuous law on it, all the while feeling desperately defeated in our own endeavors. By doing so, the sin present within our fallen flesh becomes more and more aroused to assert itself. The more it asserts itself, the more law we place on it, mustering up more determination and self-imposed will. What if instead, though, we just do what the Bible says and simply count ourselves as dead to sin? Then, in the moment the flesh tries to rise up, we remember, "Oh yes, I am certain I died to that already!" Then, we move on reminding ourselves that we have been created and endowed with God's own righteousness and holiness and that we are free from sin and the law.

Present your bodies as a living sacrifice.

In Romans 12:1, Paul urges us as believers to present our bodies as a living sacrifice, holy and pleasing to God as our spiritual act of worship.

> **Romans 12:1-2 -** [1] Therefore, I urge you, brothers, in view of God's mercy, to offer your bodies as living sacrifices, holy and pleasing to God—this is your spiritual act of worship. [2] Do not conform any longer to the pattern of this world, but be transformed by the renewing of your mind. Then you will be able to test and approve what God's will is—his good, pleasing and perfect will.

At first glance, a "living sacrifice" seems to be a contradiction in terms. Biblically speaking, a sacrifice is something that is intended to be put to death as an offering to God. Notice specifically what is being offered here as a sacrifice ... *our bodies*. This is obviously not saying that we are to physically put our own bodies to death; that is why offering our bodies to God is called a "*living sacrifice.*" However, it is also clear that we are not being instructed to fix something that is intended to be sacrificed.

When we became a believer, the change made inside of us was internal and eternal. It is our fleshly mind and thinking patterns that currently fight against us. The changes we attempt to force through the self-effort of flesh on the outside at correcting character and behavior have no real long term effect. Only the work of God on the inside of us can truly transform us to the full knowledge of Christ, thus finding its eventual outward expression in the character and conduct of our flesh. Therefore, as our carnal minds are intentionally renewed in the knowledge of the truth of what has already taken place inside of us, and as we learn to walk in that truth, the activity of our flesh is directly impacted.

Let go of human effort.

Galatians 3:1-5 [1] You foolish Galatians! Who has bewitched you? Before your very eyes Jesus Christ was clearly portrayed as crucified. [2] I would like to learn just one thing from you: Did you receive the Spirit by observing the law, or by believing what you heard? [3] Are you so foolish? After beginning with the Spirit, are you now trying to attain your goal by human effort? [4] Have you suffered so much for nothing—if it really was for nothing? [5] Does God give you his Spirit and work miracles among you because you observe the law, or because you believe what you heard?

A true Christ follower will understand that we are saved by grace through faith, and that our salvation does not come from us, but is imparted to us as a free gift from God. Frequently, once we gain that confidence, however, we think the rest of our Christian journey is up to us, especially as it pertains to living righteously. We begin by the spirit, but then turn to our own human self-effort. Because the will and bend of our flesh is to remain independent from God, our flesh likes to be the one in the driver's seat; it likes to be in control. Our flesh finds familiarity with trying to live righteously apart from divine influence. If you think about it, this is the way we lived before Christ. We tried by ourselves to be good enough and strong enough to please God. When we finally realized we weren't able to do that, we let go of our self-effort and turned to God for help. However, frequently, after we get the help, especially if we are unaware of the work of regeneration on the inside, our flesh reverts back to old patterns of striving for perfection through self-effort. Unfortunately, many times, the firm grip of religion tends to feed this fleshly craving, giving us the false impression of being right with God through a man-made artificial system of independent religious activity.

We must remember that Romans 1:17 tells us the righteousness found in the good news of Jesus Christ comes *from God*, by faith, from first to last. It is God alone that produces true righteousness in and through us. He deposited this righteousness in us when He perfectly created us new in His own image of righteousness and holiness at salvation. Therefore, with that understanding, in faith, we have to be brave enough to let go of our fleshly control issues, put hands and feet in the air, and give up all our self-efforts toward righteousness. I know for many of us, even reading that statement brings a huge twinge of "... yes, but ...;" I believe that response is exactly that flesh tendency toward independence still driving our doubts. However, we must realize that we will only experience the fruit of true righteousness flowing through our lives as we learn to let go and completely rely upon the internal work of Christ in us.

Take your thoughts captive.

2 Corinthians 10:3-6 - [3] For though we live in the world, we do not wage war as the world does. [4] The weapons we fight with are not the weapons of the world. On the contrary, they have divine power to demolish strongholds. [5] We demolish arguments and every pretension that sets itself up against the knowledge of God, and we take captive every thought to make it obedient to Christ. [6] And we will be ready to punish every act of disobedience, once your obedience is complete.

It is crucial that we understand the battleground of the carnal mind. Our thought life plays a very critical role to our living victoriously on this earth. We have a responsibility to take our carnal thoughts captive, making each of them obedient to Christ. It is not hard to tell what the thoughts of the flesh are and the thoughts of the spirit. Over and over in scripture, we find the Bible paints a very clear picture of the differences between the two. Therefore, when we find our thinking patterns setting themselves up against what we already know about God's righteousness, we can quickly recognize that as the flesh and take the thought captive, making it obedient to the righteousness of Christ on the inside.

Set your mind on things above.

Not only do we take captive the thoughts we know to be representing the cravings and desires of our flesh, we actively replace those thoughts with the true things of the Spirit of God.

Colossians 3:1-10 - [1] Since, then, you have been raised with Christ, set your hearts on things above, where Christ is seated at the right hand of God. [2] Set your minds on things above, not on earthly things. [3] For you died, and your life is now hidden with Christ in God. [4] When Christ, who is your life, appears, then you also will appear with him in glory. [5] Put to death, therefore, whatever belongs to your earthly nature: sexual immorality, impurity, lust, evil desires and greed, which is idolatry. [6] Because of these, the wrath of God is coming. [7] You used to walk in these ways, in the life you once lived. [8] But now you must rid yourselves of all such things as these: anger, rage, malice, slander, and filthy language from your lips. ⁹ Do not lie to each other, since you have *taken off your old self* with its practices ¹⁰ and have *put on the new self*, which is being renewed in knowledge in the image of its Creator.

2 Corinthians 4:16-18 - ¹⁶ Therefore we do not lose heart. Though outwardly we are wasting away, yet inwardly we are being renewed day by day. ¹⁷ For our light and momentary troubles are achieving for us an eternal glory that far outweighs them all. ¹⁸ So we fix our eyes not on what is seen, but on what is unseen. For what is seen is temporary, but what is unseen is eternal.

Hebrews 12:1-3 – ¹ Therefore, since we are surrounded by such a great cloud of witnesses, let us throw off everything that hinders and the sin that so easily entangles, and let us run with perseverance the race marked out for us. ² Let us fix our eyes on Jesus, the author and perfecter of our faith, who for the joy set before him endured the cross, scorning its shame, and sat down at the right hand of the throne of God. ³ Consider him who endured such opposition from sinful men, so that you will not grow weary and lose heart.

Finally, make sure of your salvation.

Before our salvation, we had a sinful nature. Therefore, the presence of sin felt natural, common, and familiar to us. However, when we become a born-again new creation in Christ, we were eternally changed. We no longer have that sin nature inside of us, and we are no longer sinners. This doesn't mean that sin in our flesh will not present itself at times seeking dominance. Obviously, if the apostle Paul dealt with this struggle, then you and I will too. But as Paul said, "It is no longer I who sin, but sin that lives in my flesh." Therefore, after receiving Christ and becoming born again, sin should feel different to us than it did before we were saved. It will feel unnatural, or contrary, to our new nature because it is no longer who we are.

The word of God is clear that if we are a born again new creation in Christ, we will not be able to live in a continuous state of sin (1 John 2:3-6; 3:4-10; 4:20; 5:18; Galatians 5:19-21). Therefore, if we are dealing with full enslavement to sin in a given area, the Bible encourages us to do everything possible to make sure that our calling and election are sure.

> **2 Peter 1:3-11** - [3] His divine power has given us everything we need for life and godliness through our knowledge of him who called us by his own glory and goodness. [4] Through these he has given us his very great and precious promises, so that through them you may participate in the divine nature and escape the corruption in the world caused by evil desires. [5] For this very reason, make every effort to add to your faith goodness; and to goodness, knowledge; [6] and to knowledge, self-control; and to self-control, perseverance; and to perseverance, godliness; [7] and to godliness, brotherly kindness; and to brotherly kindness, love. [8] For if you possess these qualities in increasing measure, they will keep you from being ineffective and unproductive in your knowledge of our Lord Jesus Christ. [9] But if anyone does not have them, he

is nearsighted and blind, and has forgotten that he has been cleansed from his past sins. [10] Therefore, my brothers, be all the more eager to make your calling and election sure. For if you do these things, you will never fall, [11] and you will receive a rich welcome into the eternal kingdom of our Lord and Savior Jesus Christ.

Remember, as a re-born child of God, we have been given everything we need for life and godliness. Even better, because of the work already done within us as spirit, God has enabled us to participate in His own divine nature. Evidence of this is a life that is increasing in faith, goodness, knowledge, self-control, perseverance, godliness, brotherly kindness, and love. If you see your life going in another direction, something is wrong. Seek the Lord, and search your heart. Ask the Holy Spirit to show you if you are depending on anything other than the sacrificial blood of Christ shed on the cross for your redemption and eternal salvation. If so, repent and turn to Him.

1 Peter 4:5-6 - [5] But they will have to give account to him who is ready to judge the living and the dead. [6] For this is the reason the gospel was preached even to those who are now dead, so that they might be judged according to men in regard to the body, but live according to God in regard to the spirit.

"Now we see but a poor reflection as in a mirror; then we shall see face to face. Now I know in part; then I shall know fully, even as I am fully known."
1 Corinthians 13:12

CHAPTER 11

MIRROR, MIRROR ON THE WALL

What is the first thing you did when you got up this morning? Whatever it is, it's probably pretty much the same thing every day. Most of us have our own special routine to get us going in the mornings. Perhaps, you make your bed first, then brush your teeth, and jump in the shower. For many, it involves a strong cup of coffee at some point. The purpose of our morning ritual is to prepare us for the day's events. For almost everyone, our morning routine involves at least some time in front of a mirror. Can you imagine if we all went to work one day without taking even one moment to glance in a mirror? Our hair would be sticking out everywhere. Our clothes would look disheveled. My point is this, most of us wouldn't dream of leaving our homes for work in the morning without spending at least a few moments in front of a mirror ... "Mirror, Mirror on the wall, who's the fairest of them all?" Real mirrors do not lie.

What is the purpose of a mirror?

A mirror gives us a reflection of who we are. Mirrors work by simply reflecting light. Some mirrors reflect the light only from the surface, while others allow the light to penetrate through the exterior surface so that it will reflect off of the inside. The quality of a mirror is determined by the amount of light reflected, how the wavelengths are being filtered out, and whether or not the reflected image is being distorted in any way?

Consider these three questions:

- When you look into a mirror, what image do you see staring back at you?

- What is the source of that reflected image?

- What kind of mirror are you looking into?

In which mirror do you find your true identity?

There are 3 different types of mirrors in which we might choose to spend our time.

The Natural Mirror

This mirror is the type of mirror that only reflects light from the surface. Unfortunately, most days we tend to spend much more time looking into this mirror than others. The natural mirror has the ability to reflect the natural image of our fallen flesh. This mirror is severely misleading because it prevents us from seeing the full truth of who we really are in Christ. In this mirror, we see the lines and wrinkles of age constantly illuminating the secrets of our personal failures and disappointments. This mirror may tell us that our identity is in things that have happened to us, such as our past, our lack of achievements, negative words that have been spoken over us by the people we love. In this mirror, we see the daily struggle of our flesh – its bend toward sin, its cravings and desires. This mirror rarely, if ever, provides encouragement; rather, it points out our weaknesses and flaws again and again. This mirror typically makes us feel defeated, worthless, hopeless, and insignificant. It veils us from God's truth about our TRUE IDENTITY as a child of God. As we spend time in it, we constantly seek to improve the image we see staring back at us. We quickly throw on some more makeup ... add some anti-wrinkle creams ... dye our hair a different color ... all in an attempt to make the image we see more appealing than what it really is. Nevertheless, this mirror has no ability to change us. When we get up the next morning, we have to go through the routine all over again.

We must remember that the Natural Mirror only looks at the surface, and what is on the surface is temporary and fleeting (2 Cor. 4:16-18). Spending any amount of time scrutinizing the image we see in this mirror does not bring about genuine holiness. All the things we might do to try to change the image we see in this mirror will have no long-term effect because the flesh that is reflected from it is still fallen. Remember, the Apostle Paul tells us in Romans 7:18 that "Nothing good lives in my flesh!" That means we can spend hours and hours in front of this mirror trying to change something in order to please God, and we will never be successful simply because our flesh never has, and never will have, anything good to offer to God. Instead, we must remember that the Word of God instructs us to count our flesh as dead to sin but alive to God (Rom. 6:11). We must choose to offer its members (e.g., hands, feet, mouth, eyes, etc.) as instruments of righteousness (Rom. 6:13), and offer our body as a living sacrifice holy and pleasing to God (Rom. 12:1).

It is imperative that we be aware that we are wasting our time if we are using the Natural Mirror as the source of our identity, or as a way in which we can improve upon ourselves in some way that would make God happier with whom we already are.

The Mirror of the Law

Though the Mirror of the Law is brutally honest, it comes from God and has a specific purpose. This mirror is the mirror that God uses to draw us to Christ. The reflection found in this mirror shows our natural image or sinful nature in comparison with God's perfect glory and righteousness. It reminds us that God's wrath is coming and that we will be judged in accordance with how we measure up to God's standard of righteous perfection. This mirror is a place of judgment. When we look into this mirror, we become glaringly conscious of our sin (Rom. 3:19-20).

This mirror can only reveal to us the truth of this reality; however, it has no power to change our awful appearance because it is rendered impotent by our sinful nature. Far too many of us spend our entire lives gazing into this mirror, in a constant struggle to put on the garments of our own righteousness in our best efforts to imitate the perfect standard of God's own righteousness, but we always find ourselves falling short of the mark. Blinded to our own failure, we parade ourselves in front of God in these filthy rags as if saying "God. Is this good enough? Will this be sufficient enough to escape your judgment?" But all the while, the law is being reflected back at us saying, "It's not enough! You have to be perfect! If you've missed even one area of this standard of perfection, you are guilty of missing all of it, because there is only one standard and that standard is the full and complete righteousness of God Himself." The problem is that without redemption through the shed blood of Christ, we remain enslaved to sin which makes it impossible for us to ever "get it right." God gave this mirror to us to tell us the truth about how we compare to God's righteous standard of perfection so that we could be led to receive the righteousness that comes from God through faith in Christ: the righteousness that is found at the center of the gospel, or "good news," of Jesus Christ (Rom. 1:16-17).

We must remember that though the Mirror of the Law was given to us by God, it was never intended to be used for our daily spiritual preparation. If, after our salvation, we choose to continue to spend our time steadily gazing into this mirror, we mistakenly live a life still in the flesh striving to meet God's righteous standards on our own. We fail to see, or remember, that because of the gospel and God's work of grace inside of us, God's own righteousness is already fully met in us. Therefore, after being made new in the image of God, we don't need to keep going again and again to this mirror to check out how we are doing. In Christ, we have *died to the law* so that we might belong to another; we have been *released from the law* so that we serve in the new way of the Spirit.

This brings me to the third mirror.

The Mirror of the Spirit, the Word of God - Jesus

The Mirror of the Spirit is perfect and pure and was made by God especially for believers. This mirror tells a truth that cannot be seen using the natural eye. The image found in it is spiritually discerned, requiring the Spirit of God inside of a person to reveal the absolute truth it reflects.

This mirror passes right through what is left of the fallen remnants of sin found in our flesh and penetrates deep inside to reflect our true beauty in Christ: that which is eternal and lasting, that which has been transformed by the hand of God. This mirror tells us the truth about who we really are as a child of God. It tells us what God has done in us and what His glorious plans are for us since before time began. This mirror brings encouragement, joy, peace, sanctification, freedom, life, hope, courage, strength, fulfillment, power, wisdom, and glory.

The problem is that many believers put this mirror in their attic to collect dust. They don't take it out very often to look at it, preferring to spend more of their time in front of the natural mirror of the flesh and the old Mirror of the Law. The truth is that our carnal mind can more readily accept the reflection it faces in the mirror of the flesh, because it belongs to this reflection. Therefore, the more time we spend in the mirror of the flesh, the more time we allow our carnal minds to forget what we know to be true about who we really are. The mirror of the living and active Word of God, however, helps us make these distinctions more clear.

Hebrews 4:12-13 - [12] For the word of God is living and active. Sharper than any double-edged sword, it penetrates even to dividing soul and spirit, joints and marrow; it judges the thoughts and attitudes of the heart. [13] Nothing in all creation is hidden from God's sight. Everything is uncovered and laid bare before the eyes of him to whom we must give account.

Notice the power of the Word of God to reveal to us the truth concerning the distinctions of our spirit and body in relation to the whole. The Word of God acts as a mirror within which we can see ourselves from God's perspective. In reading it, God is able to reveal to us those things that are of our flesh and those which are spirit, the seat of our thought patterns and the attitudes of our heart. In the New Testament, James exhorts us:

> *The Word of God acts as a mirror within which we can see ourselves from God's perspective.*

James 1:22-25 - [22] Do not merely listen to the word, and so deceive yourselves. Do what it says. [23] Anyone who listens to the word but does not do what it says is like a man who looks at his face in a mirror [24] and, after looking at himself, goes away and immediately forgets what he looks like. [25] But the man who **looks intently** into the perfect law that **gives freedom**, and **continues** to do this, **not forgetting** what he has heard, but doing it—he will be blessed in what he does.

James uses this analogy of the mirror to tell us that when we go to the Mirror of the Word of God, we see a reflection of who we really are. But he cautions us *"to look intently"* (or with intention) into the *"perfect law that gives freedom"* and to *"continue to do this"* – *"not forgetting."* Look at the amazing promise that comes from spending time in this mirror: *"He will be blessed in what He does."*

But the Word of God is not only a book, it is a person Revelation 19:11-13 describes a rider on a white horse called *"Faithful and True."* Verse 13 says, *"He is dressed in a robe dipped in blood, and His name is the Word of God."* John 1:1 tells us that *"In the beginning was the Word, and the Word was with God and the Word was God."* Jesus is the Word of God and the Word of God is our mirror. So, when we look into this mirror, we should always see the light of Christ reflected back at us.

Now let's look at 2 Corinthians 3:7-18:

2 Corinthians 3:7-18 - [7] Now if the ministry that brought death, which was engraved in letters on stone, came with glory, so that the Israelites could not look steadily at the face of Moses because of its glory, fading though it was, [8] will not the *ministry of the Spirit* be even more glorious? [9] If the *ministry that condemns men is glorious* (THE LAW), how much more glorious is the *ministry that brings righteousness!* [10] For what was glorious has no glory now in comparison with the surpassing glory. [11] And if what was fading away came with glory, how much greater is the glory of that *which lasts!* [12] Therefore, since we have such a hope, we are very bold. [13] We are not like Moses, who would put a *veil over his face* to keep the Israelites from gazing at it while the radiance was fading away. [14] But their minds were made dull, for to this day the same veil remains when the old covenant is read. It has not been removed, because *only in Christ is it taken away.* [15] Even to this day when Moses is read, a veil covers their hearts. [16] But whenever anyone turns to the Lord, *the veil is taken away.* [17] Now the Lord is the Spirit, and *where the Spirit of the Lord is, there is freedom.* [18] And we, who with *unveiled* *faces* all *reflect* the *Lord's glory*, are being transformed into *his likeness* with *ever-increasing glory*, which comes from the Lord, who is the Spirit.

What reflection will we see when we look into the spiritual mirror of Jesus, the Word of God? When we look into this mirror, we will see the likeness of the very glory of God Himself who has given us his Spirit; the Spirit of freedom, the Spirit that tells us we are a child of God, a new creation (Romans 8:12-17; 2 Cor. 5:17).

This mirror reveals things that will never be seen in our natural mirrors or the mirror of the Law. Though the other two mirrors still may reveal some truth regarding our fallen flesh, we must remember that our flesh is only temporary. However, the image we see reflected back through the Mirror of the Spirit or Word of God is ETERNAL!

What does it look like to spend time in front of this mirror? Like any mirror, it is a place of preparation and readying ourselves for the day. It is a place where we teach our carnal mind to accept the truth of who we are in Christ and put our flesh down in submission to that truth. It is the place where we make the deliberate choice to fix our eyes on that which is unseen and eternal. It is a place where we allow our minds to be renewed, where we take off the old self and put on the new, and where we allow the Spirit of

God to clothe us in the beautiful wardrobe that God has given to every believer.

As we spend more and more time in this mirror, we walk away being confident and assured of its truth. We remember the realities that our reflection bears the image of the righteous and holy God, that we are endowed with God's own love, power, and self-control, that we are fully free from guilt, shame, bondage, and fear. Furthermore, in this mirror, we find hope for an eternal glory with God that He has planned for His creation before the beginning of time. We are reminded that we don't need to add or take away anything to make ourselves more presentable to God, because we have already been justified and forgiven and perfectly created by God, lacking nothing. We can look at this reflection and say with complete confidence, "I am holy as God is holy. This is not because I have done anything to make myself that way. By no means! Rather, it is solely because of the undeniable grace of God given to me by my faith in, or complete confidence and reliance upon, the work of my redeeming Messiah on the cross. I praise God because I am fearfully and wonderfully made."

At times, our carnal minds may still have difficulty accepting the full reality of what it sees in the Mirror of the Spirit, as if it is looking at a dimly lit mirror. But we can be encouraged that a day is coming when we will no longer know in part; rather, we will know fully even as we are fully known by our Savior and Lord, as we see the glorious plans of God fully unfold.

1 Corinthians 13:12 - Now we see but a poor reflection as in a mirror; then we shall see face to face. Now I know in part; then I shall know fully, even as I am fully known.

"... put on the new self, created to be like God in true righteousness and holiness."
Ephesians 4:24

CHAPTER 12

A BRAND NEW WARDROBE

After becoming a new creation in Christ, our Father knew that our old worn out "fig leaves" were not sufficient to cover our nakedness and that we desperately needed something new to wear as a reminder to ourselves, and to others around us, of the truth of the unseen. Therefore, because of His great love for us, He has gifted us with a brand new designer wardrobe. For the next portion of this chapter, let's look at a first person example of how we might daily "put on" this new spiritual wardrobe as we gaze intently into the mirror of God's word to see the beautiful reflection of Christ's glory staring back at us:

My Daily Wardrobe

The Paper Doll Princess

I am a Paper Doll Princess, and I love to dress up. Though my flesh is as worthless as paper, my true value lies on my inside where I am a royal princess, a daughter of the most High King. When I look in the mirror, I choose not to see my temporary paper features; rather, I take hold of the reality of who I am through the redeeming work of Christ, my Lord.

Today, I make a deliberate choice to "put on" the new wardrobe given to me by my Heavenly Father.

First, I put on the Lord Jesus Christ, my Savior and Redeeming Messiah, knowing that all I am and all I have is not because of anything I have done, but because of the sacrifice of His own body given for me (Romans 13:14). I have His life inside of me. I am in Him and He is in me (John 15).

Next, I put on my new self, remembering that I am a born-again child of the righteous and holy God, perfectly created in His righteous and holy image. (Eph. 4:24)

I put on the armor of light, because I know that I am a child of the light and not the darkness.

Ephesians 5:8-9 – [8] For you were once darkness, but now you are light in the Lord. Live as children of light. [9] For the fruit of the light consists in all goodness, righteousness and truth.

Romans 13:12 - The night is nearly over; the day is almost here. So let us put aside the deeds of darkness and *put on* the armor of light.

Furthermore, I add the garments of compassion, kindness, humility, gentleness and patience. These virtues come from God and are already part of my spiritual DNA.

Colossians 3:12 - Therefore, as God's chosen people, holy and dearly loved, *clothe yourselves* with compassion, kindness, humility, gentleness and patience.

Galatians 5:22-25 - [22] But the fruit of the Spirit is love, joy, peace, patience, kindness, goodness, faithfulness, [23] gentleness and self-control. Against such things there is no law. [24] Those who belong to Christ Jesus have crucified the sinful nature with its passions and desires. [25] Since we live by the Spirit, let us keep in step with the Spirit.

Next, I put on love, for I know that God has imparted to me His own perfect love, and I am, therefore, fully enabled to love others with the *same love* in which He loves me. This one virtue sums up all I am to be and do while on this earth and binds everything else I wear together in perfect unity.

Colossians 3:14 - And over all these virtues *put on love*, which binds them all together in perfect unity.

I wear a crown of beauty, the oil of gladness and joy, and a beautiful garment of praise. I am reminded that because of Christ's redeeming work, I can walk today knowing that I am beautiful in the eyes of my Lord. I am enabled to wear the sweet smelling aroma of gladness and the garment of praise to my God. I am a strong oak of righteousness that has been planted by the Lord for the display of His splendor.

Isaiah 61:1-3 – [1] The Spirit of the Sovereign Lord is on me, because the Lord has anointed me to preach good news to the poor. He has sent me to bind up the broken-hearted, to proclaim freedom for the captives and release from darkness for the prisoners, [2] to proclaim the year of the Lord's favor and the day of vengeance of our God, to comfort all who mourn, [3] and provide for those who grieve in Zion— to *bestow on them* a crown of beauty instead of ashes, the oil of gladness instead of mourning, and a garment of praise instead of a spirit of despair. They will be called oaks of righteousness, a planting of the Lord for the *display of his splendor.*

I put on the garments of salvation and robes of God's own righteousness gifted to me by His fully sufficient grace.

Isaiah 61:10 - I delight greatly in the Lord; my soul rejoices in my God. For *he has clothed me* with garments of salvation and arrayed me in a robe of righteousness, as a bridegroom adorns his head like a priest, and as a bride adorns herself with her jewels.

On top of that, I put on my spiritual armor so that I can effectively stand my ground against the devil's schemes:

❖ **The Belt of Truth** – because the truth sets me free and protects me from Satan's lies and the deception of my own flesh. Jesus is the way, the truth and the life.

❖ **The Breastplate of Righteousness** – because I understand that as a new spirit, I have been endowed with God's own righteousness. Therefore, I choose to wear His righteousness today, rather than covering myself in the filthy rags of my own righteousness generated through the synthetic self-effort of my fallen flesh. Jesus is my righteousness.

❖ **Shoes of the Gospel** – Doesn't everybody just love shoes? I put on the precious shoes of the gospel of peace, readying myself to be used by God to proclaim the truth of the good news of Jesus Christ to all whom God will lead into my path. I am reminded that my steps today are ordered by the Lord. Jesus is the good news of the gospel.

❖ **The Shield of Faith** – I take up the protective shield of faith knowing that my hope is not in those things that are seen, but in those things that are unseen. For what is seen is temporary, but what is unseen is eternal. My faith is in Christ alone.

❖ **The Helmet of Salvation** – I put on the helmet of my salvation making sure my carnal mind knows that because I have accepted Jesus as both Savior and Lord, I am completely covered by Him no matter what may come my way in this day. I have hope for an eternal inheritance that will never perish, spoil, or fade being kept for me by my heavenly Father. Jesus is my salvation and my inheritance.

❖ **The Sword of the Spirit** – Finally, I pick up the Sword of the Spirit, which is the Word of God. I acknowledge that the Word of God is living and active and written on my spiritual heart. I pray that God will bring it to my mind throughout the day as the need arises so that I can give a defense of the hope that I have within me. Jesus is the Word.

Furthermore, I count myself as dead to sin and alive to God. I offer my body as a living sacrifice, holy and pleasing to God. I put the members of my body in submission to the righteousness of God on the inside and hand them over as instruments to God to accomplish all the work which He has prepared in advance for me to do this day.

Now, I give thanks to my God for this new wardrobe and look forward to putting it on again tomorrow.

———

The more often we practice going to our new wardrobe closet as the source for our daily attire, the sooner the day will come when the tired old clothes of our fallen flesh will no longer fit, and we will begin to more readily recognize when we are wearing something that has not been designed by our Father for us to wear.

Our heavenly Father delights in seeing us wear our new clothes.

"However, as it is written: 'No eye has seen,
no ear has heard, no mind has conceived
what God has prepared for those who love him'"
1 Corinthians 2:9

CHAPTER 13

HAPPILY EVER AFTER ...

In the culmination of our truly magnificent princess' tale, we gain inexpressible joy and refuge in the notoriously grand pronouncement of our delightful eternal future with the Lord, "*...and they lived happily ever after.*" Though the primary focus of this book has been on the realities of walking in this life as a new creation in Christ Jesus, the noble journey of our true redemption story can only be properly concluded as we look toward the glorious eternal hope we have as the blessed Redeemed of the Lord.

Revelation 22:12-13 - "[12]Behold, I am coming soon! My *reward* is with me, and I will give to everyone according to what he has done. [13]I am the Alpha and the Omega, the First and the Last, the Beginning and the End."

The future reward we have awaiting us, through the comprehensive redeeming work of our Messiah, is extraordinarily beyond our greatest imaginations. We have already learned that the spirit has been given to us as a deposit guaranteeing that there is so much more to come. We have also expended much of our focus on learning about the flesh, what it is, and how to be effective in our struggle against it while walking in this life. However, we have also learned the final truth concerning our flesh is that it is destined to die and return to dust. God has something brand new, more glorious than we can ever conceive to take its place; but, that's not the end of our glorious Redemption story.

Remember the final step in the redemption process is: *That which was lost must be returned.* There is something else that we have not yet mentioned that was also directly impacted by the punitive consequences of sin in the garden. We were not the only ones that were altered from our original design, and we were not the only ones that received the judgment of death.

Genesis 3:17-19 - [17]To Adam he said, "Because you listened to your wife and ate from the tree about which I commanded you, 'You must not eat of it,' *"Cursed is the* *ground because of you;* through painful toil you will eat of it all the days of your life. ¹⁸ It will produce thorns and thistles for you, and you will eat the plants of the field. ¹⁹ By the sweat of your brow you will eat your food until you return to the ground, since from it you were taken; for dust you are and to dust you will return."

EARTH/CREATION AFTER THE FALL
"Cursed is the Ground because of you."

Take a look at the following passage in Romans pertaining to the current state of the existing heavens and the earth as it relates to God's plan of redemption.

Romans 8:18-25 - ¹⁸ I consider that our present sufferings are not worth comparing with the *glory that will be revealed in us.* ¹⁹ The *creation waits in eager expectation* for the sons of God to be revealed. ²⁰ For the *creation was subjected to frustration*, not by its own choice, but by the will of the one who subjected it, in hope ²¹ that the *creation* *itself will be liberated from its bondage to decay* and *brought into the glorious freedom of the children of God.* [22] We know that the *whole creation has been groaning as in the pains of childbirth right up to the present time.* [23] Not only so, but we ourselves, who have the *firstfruits of the Spirit,* groan inwardly as we *wait eagerly for our adoption as sons, the redemption of our bodies.* [24] For in this hope we were saved. But hope that is seen is no hope at all. Who hopes for what he already has? [25] But if we hope for what we do not yet have, we wait for it patiently.

Sometimes, we are so focused on the concerns of our own brokenness that we forget the rest of God's creation was also subjected to frustration at the time of the fall. It was broken, not by its own choice, but by ours. The passage above paints an amazing picture of all of God's creation waiting in *eager expectation* for the sons of God to be revealed. Why is the Earth so expectant for the sons of God to be revealed? Verse 21 tells us that it waits *in hope* that the creation itself will be *liberated from its bondage to decay* and brought into *the glorious freedom of the children of God.* God has a plan for redeeming the earth too. He has a plan for it sharing in the same freedom that we currently experience as a new creation in Christ Jesus. Verse 22 says that the creation is groaning as in the pains of child birth right now, and we also groan in the same way having the firstfruits of God's redemptive work already accomplished in our newly created spirit, yet still longing for the future redemption of our bodies.

The Heaven's and the Earth are the final recipients of Christ's redeeming work on the cross.

Acts 3:19-21 - [19] Repent, then, and turn to God, so that your sins may be wiped out, that times of refreshing may come from the Lord, [20] and that he may send the Christ, who has been appointed for you—even Jesus. [21] He must remain in heaven *until the time comes for God to restore everything, as he promised long ago through his holy prophets.*

God has planned from the very beginning to restore *everything* that was lost due to our sin. Not only have we received a brand new spirit, and not only will we receive a brand new body, but God has also promised us a brand new home of righteousness, the glorious redemption of the heavens and the earth.

The redemption of the heavens and the earth is not a theme we hear only in New Testament writings; it is also spoken of frequently by the Old Testament prophets as well. The prophet Isaiah, for example, tells us that the Lord will bring comfort to Zion, making her deserts like Eden and her wastelands like the garden of the Lord. He shares that before that can happen, the present heavens and earth have to die. Does that sound familiar? We have already learned that everything must die before it can be made new. This passage goes on to say that the ransomed of the Lord will return and enter Zion with singing. Who are the ransomed of the Lord? It is those of us who have accepted the ransom price of Christ's blood that was paid for our redemption.

> **Isaiah 51:3, 6, 11** - ³ The Lord will surely comfort Zion and will look with compassion on all her ruins; he will make her deserts like Eden, her wastelands like the garden of the Lord. Joy and gladness will be found in her, thanksgiving and the sound of singing. ... ⁶ Lift up your eyes to the heavens, look at the earth beneath; the heavens will vanish like smoke, the earth will wear out like a garment and its inhabitants die like flies. But my salvation will last forever, my righteousness will never fail. ... ¹¹ The *ransomed* of the Lord will return. They will enter Zion with singing; everlasting joy will crown their heads. Gladness and joy will overtake them, and sorrow and sighing will flee away.

Where are the ransomed of the Lord going to return? The next few chapters begin to describe the new heavens and the new earth that God will create. The description of the new Zion found in Isaiah's writings is amazingly parallel to the New Testament description of the new heavens and new earth, the future home of the righteous, found in the last two chapters of the Bible, Revelation 21 & 22.

> **Isaiah 65:17-19** - "¹⁷ Behold, *I will create new heavens and a new earth*. The former things will not be remembered, nor will they come to mind. ¹⁸ But be glad and rejoice forever in what I will create, for I will create Jerusalem to be a delight and its people a joy. ¹⁹ I will rejoice over Jerusalem

and take delight in my people; the *sound of weeping and of crying will be heard in it no more.*

The Eternal Inheritance

Psalm 115:15 tells us that "The highest heavens belong to the Lord, but the earth he has given to man." The first thing we need to understand is that the New Heavens and New Earth are part of the inheritance of the saints of God. Like Abraham, we too have been given God's very precious promises for a glorious future inheritance. As a matter of fact, would it surprise you to know that the promise given to Abraham concerning his inheritance and the promise given to us concerning ours is exactly the same?

Let's start by first looking at God's promise to Abraham, specifically concerning land found in Genesis, chapters 12-13. Instead of going through the entire text, we will highlight two key verses:

Genesis 12:7 - The Lord appeared to Abram and said, "*To your offspring* I will give this land."

Genesis 13:15 - All the land that you see I will give *to you and your offspring forever.*

Notice that the land promise given to Abraham was promised not just to Abraham, but also to his offspring. Also notice the time stamp given to this promise. It was promised to Abraham and his offspring *forever*. So the first question we must consider is: *Who are Abraham's offspring?* Without examining scripture closely, it would be assumed that Abraham's offspring are specifically the Jewish people, born through the son of promise, Isaac. However, the Bible makes it clear that Abraham's offspring are not limited to his direct blood descendants, but also includes those who have the same faith like Abraham, faith to believe God's word and His promises. Those with that same faith are, therefore, credited like Abraham with God's righteousness, and therefore, become fellow partakers of Abraham's promised inheritance.

Romans 4:11-12 - [11] And he *(Abraham)* received the sign of circumcision, a seal of the righteousness that he had by faith while he was still uncircumcised. So then, he is the *father of all who believe* but have not been circumcised, *in order that righteousness might be credited to them.* [12] And he is also the father of the circumcised who not only are circumcised but who also walk in the footsteps of the faith that our father Abraham had before he was circumcised.

Romans 4:18-25 – [18] Against all hope, Abraham in hope believed and so became the father of many nations, just as it had been said to him, "So shall your offspring be." [19] Without weakening in his faith, he faced the fact that his body was as good as dead—since he was about a hundred years old—and that Sarah's womb was also dead. [20] Yet he did not waver through unbelief regarding the promise of God, but was strengthened in his faith and gave glory to God, [21] being fully persuaded that God had power to do what he had promised. [22] This is why "it was credited to him as righteousness." [23] The words "it was credited to him" *were written not for him alone,* [24] *but also for us, to whom God will credit righteousness* — for us who believe in him who raised Jesus our Lord from the dead. [25] He was delivered over to death for our sins and was raised to life for our justification.

Paul clearly explains that Abraham is the Father of *all who believe* with the same faith that Abraham had when he simply believed God at His word and obeyed.

Paul's letter to the Galatians continues to reaffirm the point that we are Abraham's children or offspring because of faith, and also asserts that because this is true, we are, therefore, enabled to share in Abraham's promised inheritance.

Galatians 3:5-9 - [5] Does God give you his Spirit and work miracles among you because you observe the law, or because you believe what you heard? [6] Consider Abraham: "He believed God, and it was credited to him as righteousness." [7] Understand, then, that *those who believe are children of Abraham.* [8] The Scripture foresaw that God would justify the Gentiles by faith, and announced the gospel in advance to Abraham: "All nations will be blessed through you." [9] *So those who have faith are blessed along with Abraham, the man of faith.*

Galatians 3:13-14 - [13] Christ redeemed us from the curse of the law by becoming a curse for us, for it is written: "Cursed is everyone who is hung on a tree." [14] *He redeemed us in order that the blessing given to Abraham might come to the Gentiles through Christ Jesus, so that by faith we might receive the promise of the Spirit.*

Galatians 3:26-29 - [26] You are all sons of God through faith in Christ Jesus, [27] for all of you who were baptized into Christ have clothed yourselves with Christ. [28] There is neither Jew nor Greek, slave nor free, male nor female, for you are all one in Christ Jesus. [29] *If you belong to Christ, then you are Abraham's seed, and heirs according to the promise.*

It is clear that because of faith, we are Abraham's offspring and heirs to the promises that God made to him. The next question then arises: *What was the inheritance promised to Abraham that pertains also to us?* Let's go back to Romans 4 for this answer.

Romans 4:13 - It was not through law that Abraham and his offspring received the promise *that he would be heir of the world*, but through the righteousness that comes by faith.

This verse clearly states that Abraham and his offspring (those who have faith like Abraham to believe) were promised that they (we) would inherit the world. However, there is no specific scripture in Genesis that explicitly tells Abraham that he will inherit the world. So where does this concept originate?

Abraham was promised the land that he saw when he looked north, south, east, and west. But did Abraham ever actually receive his inheritance? The answer to this question is found in Genesis 15:

Genesis 15:4-6 – [4] Then the word of the Lord came to him: "This man will not be your heir, but a son coming from your own body will be your heir." [5] He took him outside and said, "Look up at the heavens and count the stars—if indeed you can count them." Then he said to him, "So shall your offspring be." [6] Abram believed the Lord, and he credited it to him as righteousness. [7] He also said to him, "I am the Lord, who brought you out of Ur of the Chaldeans to give you this land to take possession of it." [8] But Abram said, "O Sovereign Lord, how can I know that I will gain possession of it?"

Genesis 15:9-11 continues with a covenant that God made, swearing by Himself to Abraham that He would be faithful in keeping His promise.

Genesis 15:12-15 – [12] As the sun was setting, Abram fell into a deep sleep, and a thick and dreadful darkness came over him. [13] Then the Lord said to him, "Know for certain that your descendants will be strangers in a country not their own, and they will be enslaved and mistreated four hundred years. [14] But I will punish the nation they serve as slaves, and afterward they will come out with great possessions. [15] *You, however, will go to your fathers in peace and be buried at a good old age.*

Though the promise God made concerning the land was given to Abraham and to his descendants, it was over 400 years before any of Abraham's direct descendants actually possessed even a piece of that promised land. Abraham certainly did not enjoy it, nor did Isaac or Jacob who were also sons of promise.

Hebrews 11 also speaks of this promised inheritance, and clearly explains why Abraham has not yet received what was promised. This passage begins with what is frequently quoted by Christians as the very definition of faith:

> **Hebrews 11:1-2** – [1] Now faith is being sure of what we hope for and certain of what we do not see. [2] This is what the ancients were commended for.

Many of us focus on the aspect of *faith* found in this chapter, which is obviously a major point. But what we sometimes miss is seeing that the faith, spoken of in this passage, specifically pertains to our promised inheritance.

> **Hebrews 11:6** - And without faith it is impossible to please God, because anyone who comes to him must believe that *he exists* and that *he rewards* those who earnestly seek him.

Notice the two points that are critical to our faith ... that *God exists* and that *God rewards*. This passage continues with an incredible list of Old Testament patriarchs who exercised their faith by acting in response to what God told them, trusting that God's reward would accompany their faith. They put their hope in what is unseen and eternal. We won't go through all of them, but I'd like to highlight a couple of key passages here:

Hebrews 11:8-10 - [8] By faith Abraham, when called to go to a place *he would later receive as his inheritance,* obeyed and went, even though he did not know where he was going. [9] By faith he made his home in the promised land like a stranger in a foreign country; he lived in tents, as did Isaac and Jacob, who were heirs with him of the same promise. [10] For *he was looking forward to the city with foundations, whose architect and builder is God.*

Abraham was called to go to a place that he would *later receive as his inheritance.* But we already saw in Genesis 15:15 that he died before ever receiving the fulfillment of the promise. However, notice what Abraham was actually looking toward in verse 10 ... *a city with foundations, whose architect and builder is God.*

Hebrews 11:11-12 - [11] By faith Abraham, even though he was past age—and Sarah herself was barren—was enabled to become a father because he considered him faithful who had made the promise. [12] And so from this one man, and he as good as dead, came descendants as numerous as the stars in the sky and as countless as the sand on the seashore.

It is the basis for all of our faith that we, like Abraham, consider Him faithful who has made the promise.

Hebrews 11:13-16 - [13] All these people were still living by faith when they died. *They **did not receive** the things promised; they only saw them and welcomed them from a distance.* And they admitted that they were aliens and strangers on earth. [14] People who say such things show that they are *looking for a country of their own.* [15] If they had been thinking of the country they had left, they would have had opportunity to return. [16] Instead, they were longing for a *better country—a heavenly one.* Therefore God is not ashamed to be called their God, for he has *prepared a city for them.*

We tend to think of the Promised Land as being the current land of Israel and the land that Joshua and the Israelites went in to conquer after the Exodus. That is not untrue; however, the Promised Land is not limited to that. These faithful patriarchs were not looking simply for physical land that they could occupy. They were looking for something even better – a holy city.

The next few verses in Hebrews 11 continue with a long list of Old Testament patriarchs who were commended for their faith: Isaac, Jacob, Joseph, Moses, as well as David, Samuel and the prophets, among many others. But the passage says none of them received the things promised.

Hebrews 11:39 - These were all commended for their faith, yet none of them received what had been promised.

There is a major point here. *None of them* received what had been promised; not even David, who was King of Israel, nor Samuel and the prophets who lived in the land of Israel after it had been taken for God's people. Furthermore, the land was promised to these descendants *forever* as an inheritance. Even today, we can see that the current country of Israel only stretches across a small portion of the land described in the Old Testament as the promised land, and the modern day Jewish people are doing everything they can even to hang on to what they have. Therefore, the promise to Abraham concerning land appears to be much bigger than the current land we now know as the "Promised Land."

Continuing with the final verse in Hebrews 11, the writer explains the reason these patriarchs, including Abraham, have not yet received what was promised.

> **Hebrews 11:40** - God had planned something better *for us* so that only together *with us* would they be made perfect.

These great patriarchs of our faith still have not received what was promised. Instead, they, like the earth, are also patiently waiting for all the sons *(and daughters)* of God to come in so that they together with us will be made perfect.

Now, let's go a little further into Hebrews, chapter 12, to find this holy city for which we are all waiting:

> **Hebrews 12:18-24** - [18] You have not come to a mountain that can be touched and that is burning with fire; to darkness, gloom and storm; [19] to a trumpet blast or to such a voice speaking words that those who heard it begged that no further word be spoken to them, [20] because they could not bear what was commanded: "If even an animal touches the mountain, it must be stoned." [21] The sight

was so terrifying that Moses said, "I am trembling with fear." ²² But you have come *to Mount Zion, to the heavenly Jerusalem, the city of the living God.* You have come to thousands upon thousands of angels in joyful assembly, ²³ to the church of the firstborn, whose names are written in heaven. You have come to God, the judge of all men, to the *spirits of righteous men made perfect,* ²⁴ to Jesus the mediator of a new covenant, and to the sprinkled blood that speaks a better word than the blood of Abel.

The Promised Land and the city whose architect and builder is God are one and the same; it is the new Jerusalem which is described as coming down out of heaven spoken of in Revelation 21 and 22, and prophesied long ago by Isaiah:

Revelation 21:1-7,10 – ¹ Then I saw a new heaven and a new earth, for the first heaven and the first earth had passed away, and there was no longer any sea. ² I saw the Holy City, the new Jerusalem, coming down out of heaven from God, prepared as a bride beautifully dressed for her husband. ³ And I heard a loud voice from the throne saying, "Now the dwelling of God is with men, and he will live with them. They will be his people, and God himself will be with them and be their God. ⁴ He will wipe every tear from their eyes. There will be no more death or mourning or crying or pain, for the *old order of things has passed away.*" ⁵ He who was seated on the throne said, "*I am making everything new!*" Then he said, "Write this down, for these words are trustworthy and true." ⁶ He said to me: "It is done. I am the Alpha and the Omega, the Beginning and the End. To him who is thirsty I will give to drink without cost from the spring of the water of life. ⁷ He who overcomes will *inherit all this,* and I will be his

God and he will be my son. ... [10] And he carried me away in the Spirit to a mountain great and high, and showed me the Holy City, Jerusalem, *coming down out of heaven from God.*

Like everything else that is to be redeemed by Christ, the old has to die before the new can come - *"for the first heaven and earth had passed away."* (Rev. 21:1)

Now let's return to Hebrews 12 to see how this will happen.

Hebrews 12:26-29 - [26] At that time his voice shook the earth, but now he has promised, "Once more I will shake not only the earth but also the heavens." [(Haggai 2:6)] [27] The words "once more" indicate the removing of what can be shaken—that is, created things—so that what cannot be shaken may remain. [28] Therefore, since we are receiving a kingdom that cannot be shaken, let us be thankful, and so worship God acceptably with reverence and awe, [29] for our "God is a consuming fire."

2 Peter, Chapter 3, is another great passage of scripture describing the future destruction of the current heavens and earth and God's plan to once again replace the old with something brand new.

2 Peter 3:2-13 - [2] I want you to recall the words spoken in the past by the holy prophets and the command given by our Lord and Savior through your apostles. [3] First of all, you must understand that in the last days scoffers will come, scoffing and following their own evil desires. [4] They will say, "Where is this 'coming' he promised? Ever since our fathers died, everything goes on as it has since the beginning of creation." [5] But they deliberately forget that long ago by God's word the heavens existed and the earth was formed out of water and by water. [6] By these waters also the world of that time was deluged and destroyed. [7] *By the same word the present heavens and earth are reserved for fire, being kept for the day of judgment and destruction of ungodly men.* [8] But do not forget this one thing, dear friends: With the Lord a day is like a thousand years, and a thousand years are like a day. [9] The Lord is not slow in keeping his promise, as some understand slowness. He is patient with you, not wanting anyone to perish, but everyone to come to repentance. [10] But the day of the Lord will come like a thief. The *heavens will disappear with a roar*; the *elements will be destroyed by fire*, and *the earth and everything in it will be laid bare.* [11] Since everything will be destroyed in this way, what kind of people ought you to be? You ought to live holy and godly lives [12] as you look forward to the day of God and speed its coming. That day will bring about the destruction of the heavens by fire, and the elements will melt in the heat. [13] But *in keeping with his promise we are looking forward to a new heaven and a new earth, the home of righteousness.*

The description of the New Heaven and New Earth, found in both Isaiah's writings as well as Revelation 21 & 22, speaks of a place where there is no death, or mourning, or crying, or pain. The word says that on the day we enter this new home of righteousness, our eternal Father will wipe every tear from our eye. The old order of things will have passed away, and the redeeming work of Christ will culminate in a splendid celebration of Christ's finished work and in our own coronation with a marvelously stunning crown of righteousness. Then once again, as in Eden, our God will make His dwelling with men, and He will come and live with us in the land of our inheritance forever.

NEW HEAVENS AND NEW EARTH
Future Home of the Redeemed

And He who was seated on the throne said, "Behold, I am making *everything* new!" (Rev. 21:5)

GOD'S PLAN OF REDEMPTION
"Behold, I am Making Everything New"
Revelation 21:5

"It is for freedom that Christ has set us free.
Stand firm, then, and do not let yourselves be
burdened again by a yoke of slavery."
Galatians 5:1

CHAPTER 14

UNTIL THEN, STAND FIRM!

For some of you, this book may have simply served as a reaffirmation of the things you already knew in the Lord. For others, I pray it has perhaps opened your eyes to a brand new way to live and walk in the spirit. But either way, we must always be on guard against Satan's schemes and the human wisdom of this world.

Our enemy knows that a church of saints walking in the truth of the regenerating work of God inside of us is a potentially lethal blow to the kingdom of darkness. We can expect him to do whatever he can to entice us away from our new found freedom in the

Lord. He will try to capitalize on the desired independence of our fallen flesh by putting burdens of law and judgment in our laps. He will attempt to draw our attention again and again back to the mirror of our fallen flesh, preventing us from seeing the reflection of God's glory found in our true identity. Perhaps, he will even use well-intended men and women of the Christian faith to impose the religious traditions of men and empty human philosophy to deter us from our course.

Paul warns us of this potential:

Colossians 2:6-8; 16-23 - [6] So then, just as you received Christ Jesus as Lord, continue to live in him, [7] rooted and built up in him, strengthened in the faith as you were taught, and overflowing with thankfulness. [8] See to it that no one takes you captive through hollow and deceptive philosophy, which depends on human tradition and the basic principles of this world rather than on Christ. ... [16] Therefore do not let anyone judge you by what you eat or drink, or with regard to a religious festival, a New Moon celebration or a Sabbath day. [17] These are a shadow of the things that were to come; the reality, however, is found in Christ. [18] Do not let anyone who delights in false humility and the worship of angels disqualify you for the prize. Such a person goes into great detail about what he has seen, and his unspiritual mind puffs him up with idle notions. [19] He has lost connection with the Head, from whom the whole body, supported and held together by its ligaments and sinews, grows as God causes it to grow. [20] Since you died with Christ to the basic principles of this world, why, as though you still belonged to it, do you submit to its rules: [21] "Do not handle! Do not taste!

Do not touch!"? [22] These are all destined to perish with use, because they are based on human commands and teachings. [23] Such regulations indeed have an appearance of wisdom, with their self-imposed worship, their false humility and their harsh treatment of the body, but they lack any value in restraining sensual indulgence.

Let us remain vigilant against these tactics to deceive us, not allowing anyone to throw us off course and lead us back to the place of bondage to sin and the law.

Galatians 5:1 - It is for freedom that Christ has set us free. Stand firm, then, and do not let yourselves be burdened again by a yoke of slavery.

Furthermore, let us run the race with endurance, let us fight the good fight of faith, and let us fix our eyes on the prize awaiting us as we look ahead to a crown of righteousness and our glorious future inheritance.

BIBLIOGRAPHY

[a]Strong, James: *The Exhaustive Concordance of the Bible: Showing Every Word of the Text of the Common English Version of the Canonical Books, and Every Occurrence of Each Word in Regular Order.* electronic ed. Ontario: Woodside Bible Fellowship, 1996, S. G1411

[b]Torres, Mike (May 27, 2009) "Neuroplasticity: Your Brain's Amazing Ability to Form New Habits" *Refocuser* RSS. Retrieved on December, 31, 2014 from http://www.refocuser.com/2009/05/neuroplasticity-your-brains-amazing-ability-to-form-new-habits/

[c]Merriam-Webster, Inc: *Merriam-Webster's Collegiate Dictionary.* Eleventh ed. Springfield, Mass.: Merriam-Webster, Inc., 2003

[d]*The Holy Bible : King James Version.* electronic ed. of the 1769 edition of the 1611 Authorized Version. Bellingham WA : Logos Research Systems, Inc., 1995, S. Re 4:11

[e]Friberg, Timothy; Friberg, Barbara; Miller, Neva F.: *Analytical Lexicon of the Greek New Testament.* Grand Rapids, Michigan: Baker Books, 2000 (Baker's Greek New Testament Library 4), S. 219

[f]Achtemeier, Paul J.; Harper & Row, Publishers; Society of Biblical Literature: *Harper's Bible Dictionary.* 1st ed. San Francisco: Harper & Row, 1985, S. 816

Unless otherwise indicated, scripture quotations are taken from the *New International Version (NIV)*. ©Copyright Zondervan, 1996, 1984, Grand Rapids, Michigan.

Front cover quotation of 2 Corinthians 5:17 is the author's paraphrase of this verse based on the NIV translation (2011) and corresponding footnote.

ABOUT THE AUTHOR

Bonny Allen Ibarra is an International Christian Event Speaker, Teacher, and Blogger. Bonny has served in ministry for more than 20 years. Her passion is to help the body of Christ discover how to walk in the amazing abundant life afforded to them through Christ.

Her inspirational messages cover gospel-centric topics such as Faith, Love, Unity, Grace, The Abundant Life, Spiritual Transformation and Identity (Regeneration), Redemption, Righteousness, Our Eternal Inheritance, and the Indwelling Life of Christ and the Holy Spirit in the Believer.

For more information about Bonny Allen Ibarra, check out her blog at http://paperdollprincess.org.

NOTE FROM THE AUTHOR

I don't know about you, but I find that the more I begin to understand my own spiritual transformation and identity in Christ, the more questions I seem to have about how the human body and spirit interact with one another and with God. I know it's probably poor form as an author to admit that I don't have all the answers; but, the fact is, I only know in part. There are many mysteries in scripture. God gives us the parts we need to understand, yet sometimes, He does not fill in all the intricate details.

Often as believers, we seek to fill in these gaps with our own philosophical logic and reasoning. I think this is very normal; however, we must be careful not to present our own philosophical logic and reasoning with the same weight as scripture. Far too often, our philosophical views can cloud our perception of what is clearly presented as Biblical truth.

When I set out to write this book, I had one objective in mind ... to write a Biblically-based book on spiritual transformation and identity. This is the mandate that I felt God had placed on my heart. The primary questions I wanted to answer were "What does it mean to be a new creation in Christ?" and "How do you 'put on' the new or walk as such?" I didn't start the book because I had all the answers; I started it because I wanted the answers and felt others might have the same questions I did.

Before I began my biblical research, I had always held the view that a person is made up of three parts – body, soul, and spirit. I wanted to see what the Bible specifically said about each one. Yet, as I began pouring through scriptures to find the answers to my questions, I found this amazing clarity spanning from Genesis to Revelation regarding the transformation of both the human body and spirit through God's plan of redemption, yet I found very little mention of the word *soul* within these contexts.

I found the word *soul* to have many different types of uses in both Old and New Testament scripture. For example, sometimes the word soul refers to a dead corpse. Sometimes, it refers to a living being or person who is alive. Sometimes it carries the idea of our whole being ... "all that is within me." Sometimes it seems to be a word that is interchanged with the human spirit. In the Psalms, it is often used to describe that deep place of yearning ...

i.e. "my soul longs for you, Oh Lord." Most often, it appears to carry the idea of life itself. Through all of its varied uses, I found it inconclusive to support that the word is strictly defined as a separate third part of an individual that houses our personality, mind, emotions, and will or sense of choice. It is certainly easy to lump these items into this very Biblical word; but, it is my opinion that to do so, perhaps puts us in danger of not seeing our true identity as the new spirit that God created us to be. I now believe that the word *soul* is best defined as a generic term, much like we would use the terms "human being" or "person." We wouldn't have a hard time calling a corpse a person, or one who is alive a person. In each case where the word soul is used, we must look at the context surrounding it to best ascertain its intended meaning.

The epistles of Paul are among my favorite and are a fantastic source for understanding spiritual identity and transformation. Paul often contrasts the realities of our newly created spirit and still fallen flesh. He always associates our true identity as our spirit, yet there seems to be little mention of the word *soul*. His letter to the Romans is perhaps one of the clearest presentations of the Gospel among all the New Testament writings, yet the word soul is not used in this letter at all. He certainly refers to renewing the mind on a regular basis, but does not specifically correlate the mind as being synonymous with the word *soul*.

In the end, I had to make an important decision. Do I force a square peg into a round whole? Do I use my own human logic and philosophical reasoning to present something which I don't see clearly defined in scripture, or do I just present scripture as is, in the way God shows it to me? Ultimately, I chose to not set forth something that I could not with absolute certainty support in scripture. I determined that if the apostle Paul didn't feel the need to slice and dice all of this up in a nice little package for us, I should probably not attempt to do so either.

With that said, I will say there are persuasive arguments that could be presented both for and against defining the word *soul* specifically as the human "mind, will and emotions." Philosophers and theologians have been trying to define the depths of our human existence for centuries. It is really hard for us, as humans sometimes, to admit that we don't know everything. Our own arguments often have the appearance of sound logic and reasoning, and perhaps they at times are; however, all I would caution is to be careful to separate the difference between what we believe to be true based on our own logic and human philosophy from what is clearly written as truth in scripture. Be careful to always give the written Word greater weight.

That being said, I believe that if you do hold the view that the soul is defined specifically as the "mind, will, and emotions" of an individual, the soul (defined as such) has not been left out of the pages of this book. If, in fact, this is the truest definition of the word, then this book has hopefully been speaking to your mind, will, and emotions from its onset. It seems to me, that regardless of any difference in how we might perceive that word, the Biblical truths presented here regarding our human flesh and spirit would still apply.

If you have been impacted from this book, or if you have questions about its content, I truly would love to hear from you. I realize that I may be opening myself up to the impossible task of responding to each email, but I promise I will try to respond to each one. You can reach me by email at: bonny@paperdollprincess.org.

Know that you are dearly loved by your Father and by me. I look forward to spending an eternal glory together with you and with our Redeeming Messiah in His glorious Kingdom.

Until then, may the grace of the Lord Jesus be with you. Amen!

CPSIA information can be obtained at www.ICGtesting.com
Printed in the USA
LVOW01s2242090415

434017LV00024B/554/P